SECOND EDITION

&KENNELS KENNELING

A guide for professionals and hobbyists

JOEL M. MCMAINS

WILEY

Wiley Publishing, Inc.

In memory of Chattan,

my Doberman friend and companion:

June 30, 1980 – February 8, 1993.

He unfailingly made this trainer look good.

Howell Book House
Copyright © 1994, 2001 Joel McMains. All rights reserved.

Published by Wiley Publishing, Inc., New York, NY

For general information on our other products and services or to obtain technical support please contact our Customer Care Department within the U.S. at 800-762-2974, outside the U.S. at 317-572-3993 or fax 317-572-4002.

Wiley also publishes its books in a variety of electronic formats. Some content that appears in print may not be available in electronic books.

Library of Congress Cataloging-in-Publication Data is available upon request from the Library of Congress.

ISBN 1-58245-151-6

Manufactured in the United States of America.

10 9 8 7 6 5

Second Edition

BOOK DESIGN BY HOLLY WITTENBERG
COVER DESIGN BY ANTHONY BAGLIANI, SOLID DESIGN

Table of Contents

Acknowledgments v

Preface vii

Section I: Home, Breeding and Training Kennels

CHAPTER 1: Designing and Building a Home Kennel 3

CHAPTER 2: The Different Needs of Breeders and Trainers 19

Section II: Boarding Kennels

CHAPTER 3: Designing and Building a Boarding Kennel 45

CHAPTER 4: Setting Up Your Business 83

CHAPTER 5: Equipment and Supplies 91

CHAPTER 6: Daily Operations 107

CHAPTER 7: Policies and Practices 121

CHAPTER 8: Record Keeping 145

CHAPTER 9: Problems and Solutions 155

CHAPTER 10: Lessons from the Best Teacher 173

Postscript 187

Canine First Aid 189

Index 195

About the Author 200

Until one is committed,
there is hesitancy,
the chance to draw back,
always ineffectiveness.
Concerning all acts of initiative
(and creation) there is
one elementary truth,
the ignorance of which
kills countless ideas
and splendid plans:
That the moment that one
definitely commits oneself,
Then Providence moves too.
All sorts of things occur
to help one that would never
otherwise have occurred.
A whole stream of events
issues from the decision,
raising in one's favor all manner
of unforeseen incidents
and meetings and material assistance,
which no man could have dreamed
would come his way.

W. H. Murray
The Scottish Himalayan Expedition

Acknowledgments

So many good people helped in this book's preparation: Ron Flath, Jo Sykes, Roger Davidson, Sharon Michael, Jim Robinson, Dale and Susan Long, Steve and Suzanne SeRine, Bill and Barb Ziegler, Darryl Dockstader, Heather Hodgkins, and John Berberick.

Special thanks to the memory of Richard Moore for his outstanding photography, and to Mack Bischoff, DVM, Blair Gustavson, DVM, Denny Peterson, DVM, all of Sheridan, Wyoming, for their technical assistance, and to Marilyn Mills of Green Acres Kennels, Rawlins, Wyoming, Cyndy Douan and Jeff White of Kingston Kennels, Kingston, Georgia, and Pat and Sandi Greenough of Country Pet Inn, Sheridan, Wyoming, for their invaluable suggestions.

I thank my friends at Howell Book House: Dominique DeVito, who proposed the revision, Amanda Sumner, whose skillful editing fulfilled my intent, and Kira Sexton, a magician at organization.

Special gratitude goes to my kenneled friends—every dog I have ever boarded—for their patience, wisdom, love and lessons, and for their company.

Most of all, I thank my special advisor, H.P.

About the Author

Joel M. McMains, an award-winning author for Howell Book House, has trained dogs professionally since "somewhere in the '70s." Along with offering professional obedience and protection training services, he operates his own boarding kennels and holds public obedience classes and training seminars.

Certified by the State of Wyoming Peace Officers' Standards and Training Commission as a Police Service K-9 Trainer and Instructor, Joel served as Chief Trainer for the Sheridan County (Wyoming) Sheriff's Department, the City of Sheridan Police Department, and search-and-rescue groups. He taught courses in K-9 selection, management, training and deployment for the Police-Science Division of Sheridan College and has testified in numerous court proceedings as an expert witness on canine behavior and training. He was also the coordinator of Sheridan County's 4-H Dog Program for twelve years.

Joel has written two other books for Howell Book House, *Dog Logic: Companion Obedience* (1992), and *Manstopper: Training a Canine Guardian* (1998). Joel now lives near Terre Haute, Indiana.

Preface

This is a book about kennels, both as a noun and a verb, transitive and intransitive. While the book's emphasis is on boarding-kennel design and operation, home kennels and breeding and training facilities are also discussed at length. *Kennels & Kenneling's* boarding section examines pluses and minuses of subjects ranging from design considerations to construction materials to day-to-day operations. The boarding section also offers ideas on advertising, public relations, record keeping, management techniques and business practices in general.

If you are looking for a book that provides definitive, "This is the only way!" answers to each and every question that can arise about kennels, however, your search must continue. To say otherwise is to imply that rock-solid principles applicable to all types of kennels exist, and that is simply not true. Kennel designs and methods of operation are not only direct reflections of purpose, they are as individual and personalized as the owner's fingerprints. A construction or management technique that is successful for one facility might result in disaster for another. There are too many variables attendant to the kennel concept for anyone to claim that any one-size-fits-all method of planning, construction, operation and decision making will be universally effective. Yes, this book offers a wealth of information for everyone from pet owners to hobbyists to professionals, but of equal importance, it provides a direction, helping you to determine questions you need to ask, raising issues you are likely to face and offering possible solutions.

One premise underlying all sections of the book is that the kennel, whatever its purpose, must be more than just adequate, yet it need not rival the Taj Mahal. We are discussing construction and operation of a facility intended for housing and catering to the needs of dogs, not people. The keys are that any kennel must be warm in winter, cool in summer, clean, dry, comfortable, safe and secure always. A second postulate is of three parts. First, that the kennel you envision is a single-story structure not larger than thirty runs; super kennel, mega-run planning is beyond this book's scope, though the management principles offered are applicable for operations of all sizes. Second, the kennel is adjacent to your home; it's on your property. Third, that the kennel operator "knows" *Canis familiaris;* he or she can read a dog, often without conscious effort.

The following thoughts are for those who are considering a career in boarding kennel management. They originally appeared under a subsection entitled "Have You Lost Your Mind?" when I first began this manuscript. The title intended a fleck of humor while making a point: Aspiring boarding kennel operators should do a bit of soul-searching before diving into the business. Running a boarding facility is not the most difficult work in the world, but in addition to being quite time-consuming, it can have negative aspects. Weekend getaways for you are out of the question, being able to count on undisturbed meals or just an evening of visiting with company is a luxury of the past, your phone will ring at strange hours and you won't always be able to get a full night's sleep. Sometimes an uninterrupted cup of coffee will seem a blessing.

In a more serious vein, any dog you board can fall prey to any of a host of illnesses, perhaps endangering other boarders and your own pets. Also, you can find yourself at physical risk from fear-driven or aggressive animals. Customers can cancel reservations at the last minute, or not let you know they have changed their plans at all, and you will occasionally witness permutations of the human-canine relationship that may cause you to have to bite your tongue. The need for maintenance and upkeep is a constant, and—unless you have reliable kennel help—you can forget what a day off is like.

Even given those drawbacks, however, and a good many more, there is nothing that many of us would rather do with our days than take care of and spend time with *Canis familiaris.* A career of managing dogs beats the daylights out of nine-to-five, commuting and office politics. Though boarding-kennel operation is not a growth industry, so long as people own dogs there will be a need for boarding kennels. In many areas of the country, boarding is largely a seasonal business. And not only is it a great way to have continual contact with man's best friend and to have constant opportunities to learn and discover, but people are actually willing to pay you to do it, too.

Home, Breeding and Training Kennels

1

Designing and Building a Home Kennel

Years ago, when I lived in Wyoming, a friend phoned one afternoon sounding like she'd just won the lottery. Would I like to see her Pomeranian's new home kennel setup? She was champagne-bubbly, and it was one of those moments when I couldn't say "No." So I drove to her house, made lots of "Ooohs" and "Ahhhs," admired the chainlink and the concrete and the sun-screens, gave her a big hug, petted her dog, grinned some more and rambled home.

Now, don't misunderstand—I was happy for my friend. Her excitement was contagious and she was trying harder than many to do right by her dog. But since the Pom was 99 percent housepet, I wondered why she had put the time, effort and money into a project that would rarely be used. I fired up my aged computer and launched its word-processing program, and typed, "Years ago, when I lived in Wyoming . . ."

Do I Really Need a Kennel?

Question number one in planning a home kennel: "Do I really need one?" Pet owners sometimes expend major resources constructing a lavish kennel when a secure fence and a sturdy dog-house or dog door would serve as well or better. Of course, if you opt for fencing an area, regardless of your preferred style it must be one that your pet cannot climb, jump, tunnel under, chew or rip apart.

Is the Kennel I Want "Legal"?

As you consider building a kennel, what type of fencing usually comes to mind? Sure, chainlink. But before looking up its current price (be seated when you do, by the way), ascertain that your planned fence or kennel won't violate building codes, covenants, ordinances or zoning regulations. It's no good to invest in an addition only to have to try to placate displeased regulators and tar-bucket-rattling neighbors later.

You should also know that some communities would classify your home as a kennel and assess an exorbitant license fee if you have more than a certain number of dogs. Other towns ban ownership of more than X dogs and some prohibit ownership of certain breeds, for instance pit bulls or other breeds that are perceived as prone to violence.

Is the Kennel I Want Right for My Dog?

As a home kennel owner, you aren't bound by the concerns that a commercial boarding kennel owner would have, such as impressing clients through landscaping, structural aesthetics and decor. For example, rather than getting fancy (and expensive), you can shade your dog's run by propping up a piece of faded plywood; boarding kennel operators doing the same thing risk giving customers a less-than-professional impression.

Your main considerations for your home kennel need to be "Will it work?" and "Will my dog be safe and comfortable?" The answers to these questions determine such things as the amount of enclosed area required, the location of the kennel, the height and type of fencing, the number of runs and the type and location of housing. For example, do you need a six-foot-high fence if you own a Dachshund? In terms of confinement, probably not. But could an intruder easily hurt or steal your pet over a fence three feet high? Probably so. In planning height, remember that confinement isn't the sole objective.

How Big Should the Kennel Area Be?

The area to enclose depends on your amount of land. If yours is a small urban lot, you might consider fencing the entire backyard and perhaps the front yard as well. Relevant factors are security, how much exercise room your dog needs and the availability of shade. If your proposed site would expose your pet to those who might tease her or worse, choose another area. If you own acreage, you may not need to fence every square foot; fencing a protected, shady location that allows running room may be adequate.

If your yard is already fenced, consider upgrading or altering an existing fence. Suppose a fence surrounding your yard is high enough to contain pooch and deter intruders, and you're considering a kennel to centralize her toilet activities. Would it be wiser just to fence off a small area of your yard for the purpose? Then, whenever your pet has taken care of business in the smaller area, you could release her into the main yard for exercise. True, your dog may still occasionally mark areas of the yard—dogs do that sort of thing, you know—but most of the leavings will be in one area, making for easier cleanups.

Where Should I Put It?

Your number one rule of kennel design should be security and comfort, not, "Where can I make this thing fit?" If your planned site would have your pet next to your property line, exposing her to possible harm, or would provide inadequate shade from summer sun or meager shelter from winter harshness, rethink.

Is your planned location close to a water source? If not, you'll have to extend a water line to the kennel or resign yourself to carrying water daily (at least) to your pet. You'll also have to drag hoses for cleaning purposes. Such considerations come under the heading of future efficiency; carrying buckets of water or dragging hoses to the kennel may seem trivial, but remember that you'll have to do these chores daily for years—and should you later acquire additional dogs, you'll be toting additional buckets.

Consider your kennel's location relative to existing electricity sources and sewer lines. Building near an electric source facilitates installation of outside lighting, an important security consideration. The desirability of sewer access is obvious, but be sure that tapping into a local system is permissible.

Another reason to situate your kennel close to electric sources is the possibility of change in your personal circumstances. You may someday find you have to leave your dogs alone for longer periods than anticipated. Nearby power can enable easier installation of water-bucket heaters and self-feeders.

You may wish to combine projects. For example, if you intend to build a workshop, storage shed or similar outbuilding, you might conserve time and money by incorporating the kennel into the structure.

What about neighbors? If one of two otherwise equal locations would be quieter for people living nearby, choose that site. Also be aware that kennel placement can affect your property values: A well-located kennel can raise them, but a poorly situated one can have a negative effect.

What Kind of Fencing and Gate Materials Should I Use?

This book is not a knowledge base about fence construction. I studied two manuals and bent the ears of several skilled and patient (and perhaps amused) friends before setting the first post. Although in some instances I describe specific details about my own solutions to fence-building problems, my main purpose in this section is to provide an overview of common fence types, materials and installations. If you are handy with tools and are so inclined, you might be able to erect your own fence, possibly using an easier method than the one I suggest below. However, risk of injury and lost time and money (not to mention wounded pride) attend any unfamiliar task, and so it may be wiser to contact professionals.

Common Materials

Chainlink is as expensive as it is durable, and installation requires skilled labor. Wood fences can be equal parts of pleasing to the eye, costly and difficult to erect. They necessitate periodic upkeep, such as painting, staining and repairing loose boards. Some are vulnerable to wind, none are fireproof, most are easily climbed and any can be a chewer's delight. Unlike installing prestretched chainlink panels, which only requires a wrench, erecting a board fence requires stakes, cord, saws, sandpaper, measuring tape, hammers, nails, levels, sawhorses, a wheelbarrow, shovels, a posthole digger and a soil-tamping bar.

I enclosed my training yards with *non-climb* (also known as *two-by-four*) wire fencing. It's durable, less expensive than wooden styles and quicker and easier to install. I fastened it to wooden posts measuring four inches square by eight feet long that had been treated against insects and moisture, to avoid having to replace them due to infestation or rot.

Sink at least 25 percent of each post's length in the ground. Setting them in concrete provides a more solid structure than does conventional bracing and tamping with dirt. You may not care to set all posts in concrete, but do so with at least gate and corner posts for stability and longevity and to prevent turning caused by the considerable tension of stretched metal fencing.

Since the tension of stretched fencing can pull gateposts out of plumb, making the top opening wider than the one at ground level, in creating my training-yard gates I set the posts in concrete and allowed it to dry overnight. Then, before attaching the fencing, I cut a length of two-by-four lumber equal to the distance between the posts plus their combined thickness. I set the board atop them and attached it with a nail at each end. This held the board in place while I drilled downward through each end and into the center of each post to accommodate six-inch-long steel bolts measuring one-half inch in diameter. Hammering the bolts through the two-by-four and into the posts completed a reasonably solid structure for handling fence tension. This may seem excessive; it may seem that nailing the two-by-four in place would do. I used to think that. Then I discovered how easily the tension of stretched fencing can bend nails.

And by the way, paint that overhead two-by-four. Bright orange. Otherwise you or a client may not notice it until after wishing you had.

After thus securing the posts' tops, I braced their centers by cutting two-by-four lumber to length, then mitering one end of each so they would attach to each upright post at a 45-degree downward angle. I nailed them to the center of each upright post, buried the exposed ends in the ground and tamped large stones around each to lessen slippage against dirt. I braced my corner posts in like fashion, after setting them in concrete.

In bracing the posts as described, I made only one mistake: My two-by-four lumber should have been four-by-four. Over time the force of the stretched fencing weakened the two-by-fours, which sagged and allowed the posts' middles to bow outward. I then discovered the joys of realigning and rebracing posts.

Tools for installing non-climb fencing, in addition to those mentioned for wooden-fence construction, include a fence stretcher (also called a *come-along*), boards and bolts for clamping the fencing material for stretching, a heavy chain to wrap around the boards and attach to the fence stretcher, a fencing tool (your hardware dealer will know what this plier-like item is), and rust-resistant steel fencing staples. Whether you prefer a wooden fence or one of the non-climb variety, consider renting rather than buying some tools, as they are costly.

Gate construction can be accomplished in many ways—I made mine from two-by-four lumber and non-climb fencing—but consider two suggestions. First, hinge each gate to its post just enough off plumb that gravity will close it. Second, use self-locking latches. Sure, you should never forget to latch a gate, just like you should never accidentally leave one open, but it's always better to be safe.

Alternatives to Chainlink

I've seen chicken-wire serve for enclosing tiny dogs, and hog or sheep panels wired to steel posts driven into the ground for large breeds. The problem with the former is it has to be stapled to boards at ground level or otherwise anchored to prevent escape, and the latter is anything but cheap. Neither is especially attractive, but that's where pet owners have it over commercial kennelers: The only person you need impress is yourself.

Lightweight woven-wire, spot-welded fencing is cheaper than non-climb, but the welds can pop during stretching and some dogs can snap them by chewing or jumping against the material. For those reasons, and the fact that moisture can break down such fencing, restrict its use to small and tiny dogs.

If you choose any kind of metal fencing, be sure the mesh size won't allow your pet either to escape or to trap her head or paws in such a way that she can't free herself.

Electric Fences

With this type of fence an owner buries a length of wire that sends signals to the dog's collar when she approaches the border. Should she come too close the collar shocks her. My objections to these fences are that they keep no one out and I've seen tough dogs learn to endure the shock for the instant it takes to rush past the perimeter.

What About Security?

Escape or intrusion: You don't want to have to deal with either, and a good kennel design and a few additional security measures can go a long way toward seeing that you rarely have to.

Basic Boundaries

If you must site your kennel along a property fence, make the side of the run that abuts the fence impenetrable. This lessens fence-fighting with neighboring dogs, and it may inhibit cretinous human types from teasing your pet. Too, were a child to put a hand through a fence into your dog's run and be injured, you could be facing a lawsuit.

A strong padlock takes care of the run gate, and a secure fence around the area completes the picture. Granted, a kennel plus a fenced yard may seem superfluous. In addition to increased security, though, it offers many options and advantages: exercise, convenience (you may not have to leash pooch to transport her to or from the kennel), and the freedom to have your pet outside without putting her in the kennel.

If you want a kennel but not a fenced yard, know that a kennel can impart a false sense of security. Lacking a fence, you've probably had to take your dog out on-leash to take care of business. Now, with a kennel, you may be lulled into believing that leashing is no longer necessary.

Wrong! You open the door to take your pet to the kennels and bang! Pupper is gone like a shot and you're trying to outrun her.

Problem Pooches

As you design your kennel, you should also keep in mind that some dogs don't necessarily "follow the rules." For instance, some dogs are escape artists—either out of joy or fear—and can climb or tunnel under the average fence. So you should build in some security measures to make sure that your dog stays safely in its enclosure.

A System for Tying—If You Must

Except for emergencies, I won't tie any dog. It not only can induce paranoia by removing flight from the fight-or-flight option, but it can also degrade trust in the owner, as the owner does the removing. If a dog must be tied, use an overhead-wire system that attaches to two widely spaced points, such as two trees or buildings. The dog's tie slides along the wire. This affords more running room and reduces the chance that the animal will wind her chain around an obstruction and strangle to death.

Countermeasures for Tunnelers

Take three steps to counter tunneling. First, plant four inches of your fence into the ground. Second, along and inside your fence, bury a flat (on its side), 18-inch-wide strip of rust-resistant mesh fencing so that the top is four inches underground. When the dog tries to dig out, she encounters the buried fencing. If she tries elsewhere, she encounters more fence. Eventually she gives up. Third, position a large slab of flagstone or similar material just above ground level under your gate. A bed of sand beneath the slab can prevent it from sinking in. Dogs who dig to escape often do so near gates, but I've yet to meet one who could tear through flagstone.

Regarding digging in general: My dog has a 10-foot by 30-foot fenced area that is part of a larger fenced yard. If she wants to dig in her small yard, not to escape but just to dig, I let her. For some dogs digging is as natural as barking, and if she enjoys that part of being a dog, why deprive her? After all, I've provided this area as hers. Digging in the larger yard, however—my yard—is *verboten*.

How Many Runs Do I Need?

A revered dog person once told me something about run construction that I've seen proven true numerous times: "Figure out how many runs you need, then double that number." My friend was acknowledging that dog owners, attracted as they are to the species, often increase their number of dogs, and it's usually easier and cheaper to erect four runs initially than to build two now and add two more later. Consider: A dog owner builds a run and then—perhaps through unforeseen circumstances—acquires a puppy. The dog likes the pup but sometimes she plays too roughly, and the owner must now decide how to house one of her pets while at work.

Though you don't want to underbuild, it's equally important to allow for expansion. I've watched more than one person evolve from pet owner to hobbyist to semiprofessional. Perhaps this will never happen to you, but always allow yourself room to grow.

Run Size

While boarding kennel runs are traditionally between three and five feet wide and are of varying lengths, home kennel runs must provide adequate exercise room to be both useful and comfortable—your dog should be able to take at least a few quick steps. Remember, they're called "runs," not "shuffles."

Though the amount of ground available at your building site may make the decision for you, consider sizing your runs as though you owned large dogs, even if your pets are small. Flexibility is the key here, because increasing existing runs' size is harder than adding new ones. True, Scotties may be the only breed for you, but that's today, and absolutes have a way of changing. A lady who started out with Beagles used to tell me, "There's no breed like them!" Today she has one aged Beagle and three young Chesapeake Bay Retrievers (she now tells me there's no breed like Chessies).

Besides, someday you may move. Sheltie-sized runs might seem more of a liability than an asset to a prospective buyer who owns Golden Retrievers. The reaction might be, "I'll have to rip those runs out and start over," which, of course, would entail more work and expense than starting from scratch, and could lead buyers to look elsewhere.

Run Surface

Concrete, gravel, and dirt are the common options. Boarding kennel owners often choose concrete simply because it's easy to clean and disinfect. But concrete is also very expensive; boarding kennels must disinfect their runs often, but do you need to sanitize your pet's quarters several times daily against every germ known to dogdom? She's going to be the only one in the kennel, and it's pretty hard for an animal to catch a disease from herself. Yes, any kennel should be periodically debugged, but does that mean you need to shoulder the expense and effort of concrete just to facilitate infrequent tasks?

Consider, too, that concrete can harm canine well-being as much as many diseases. Boarders seldom show concrete's wearing effects because they are on it for relatively short periods. A dog on concrete for many hours a week, though, year in and year out, will develop elbow calluses at least and skeletal problems at worst. Notice how your own feet, legs and back feel after standing on the unyielding surface for just a few hours, even if you wear well-constructed, comfortable shoes. Prolonged confinement on concrete eventually breaks down any animal.

Should you prefer concrete, promote runoff of liquids by sloping the pad away from your dog's rest area at a quarter inch per foot. The pad's thickness depends upon its overall size, the climate and ground stability. Seek opinions from a professional mason or driveway contractor when planning thickness and deciding whether to reinforce the pad with wire mesh.

"But can gravel or dirt be disinfected?" Up to a point, yes. You will use more disinfecting solution; since scrub brushes and squeegees are out of the question, because you will have to saturate the area and rinse it afterward. But again: How often do you need to disinfect a run that is occupied always and only by the same dog? Remember, too, that one of nature's best germ killers, sunlight, can zap many surface microbes. Disinfecting is intended for nooks and crannies sunlight can't reach, and to zap bugs that the sun's ultraviolet rays and subsequent drying don't exterminate.

Another positive about gravel is that it is easier to install than concrete. Fewer tools are required—a wheelbarrow, shovels and rakes comprise the list—and the job does not require the skill needed to pour and finish concrete. Unlike concrete, gravel is vulnerable to digging, but its impermanence can be a plus should you ever want to eliminate the kennel. Removing packed gravel is difficult, yes, but ripping out concrete can make you wish you'd never heard of the stuff. Gravel offers home kennelers a sound, practical alternative, and confinement on it is less wearing.

Of course, were the dogs allowed a vote they'd choose dirt-surfaced runs. Dirt is natural, more comfortable than any hard surface, and of utmost importance (to a dog, at least) it's a digger's paradise. The drawback to dirt runs, other than the fact that they're easy for dogs to dig, is that dirt makes for dirty dogs, especially during wet weather. That's when dirt quickly becomes mud and an adorable pet quickly becomes an adorable mudball. To envision such a pooch trotting across the living room carpet or shaking herself near the sofa will make anyone cringe. She must be bathed and dried before she can be let into the house, and by the time some long-haired breeds are dry enough to allow them inside, it's time to put them out again. Dirt runs may be okay for outdoor dogs or in arid locales, but gravel or concrete is preferable for housepets.

If you choose gravel- or dirt-surfaced runs, thwart tunnelers by following the steps in the section "Countermeasures for Tunnelers" presented earlier.

Run Fencing Materials

Rolled chainlink is well suited to run construction but, as mentioned, it's also expensive and can necessitate hiring installers. Pre-stretched chainlink panels, however, can be attached to one another using only a wrench to create a freestanding run in minutes.

Serviceable runs can be erected at less cost using non-climb fencing and wooden posts. Remembering that a run is a small fenced yard, refer to the foregoing section on fencing and gate materials for specifics about this type of material. If you choose a wooden-post-and-metal-mesh type of fencing, wherever possible configure your runs to attach the fencing to the posts on the inside of the runs to lessen opportunities for chewing.

Regardless of your fencing-style preference, top the runs with fencing for added security and make them tall enough to allow you to stand inside without stooping. Also remember that packed snow can quickly reduce effective run height and can have you walking like a question mark in a topped run or your pet scampering over an uncovered one.

Other Run Considerations

While boarding kennel runs are erected with permanence in mind, pet owners aren't bound by the principle. You have design and construction options where a kennel operator might feel constrained by convention. Of course, your runs should be secure enough that no common force can topple them, but that doesn't mean that they must be installed in a non-detachable manner. Many mass-merchandiser catalogs, as well as those of businesses offering canine specialty products, offer bolt-together chainlink panels that might be perfect not just for renters but for folks who want the option of taking the structure with them should they move.

Another consideration is that pet-kennel owners need not build using new equipment. Boarding kennel people often have little choice, since much of their chainlink is customized. When constructing my boarding kennel, however, had I been able to locate used chainlink fencing and gates of certain dimensions and degrees of slope (as well as a few other niceties), certainly I would have been tempted to grab it and would have likely saved a bundle. Before springing for new materials, check newspapers' classified sections and shoppers' guides for used fencing. Also check radio stations' for-sale-or-trade programs. As mentioned, chainlink is expensive, and while new and shiny is nice, it isn't always *that* nice.

Managing Waste Disposal

Though your number of pets can figure in the decision of how best to keep runs clean (as can public-health dictates), for most home-kennel owners a scoop designed for the purpose and a garbage can double-lined with heavy-duty trash sacks—along with taking pains to stay on good terms with the trash collectors—is often the most efficient way to remove solid wastes.

If you'd like something a little less "hands-on," consider surrounding the run pad with several inches of gravel into which urine and cleaning solutions can be hosed. It's adequate for most home-kennel setups.

If you're really ambitious—and have money to burn—you could consider building concrete-surfaced runs that empty into a sloped trough perpendicular to and beyond the run's length. This is common in boarding kennels, but unless you have several dogs and wish to go to the expense of installing a septic system into which the trough can empty, such a setup—though inarguably efficient and easy to use—represents needless additional expense, which can be considerable.

Doghouses and Other Living Quarters

The most common—and practical—forms of pet housing are a doghouse or a run attached to the house or garage, with a dog door allowing the dog to move from the house to the run.

Prefabricated Doghouses

If you decide on a doghouse consider two basic options: Placing the structure within the run, or outside the run and attaching the run to it. Placing the doghouse in the run increases security as your pet is always behind a lockable gate. But with runs lacking fencing across their tops, lessened security results if the dog can climb atop the doghouse to take a shot at going over the run. Also, placing a wooden doghouse inside a run can promote chewing, a canine option you can lessen by situating the house outside the fence and attaching the run to it. Whatever you decide about placement, be aware that heated doghouses as well as heated floor surfaces are available. Such products can be extremely valuable to those of us not living in the tropics.

Avoid one style of doghouse, however: metal. During extreme heat or cold they can be next to useless and even hazardous.

Building a Doghouse from Scratch

Though prefabricated doghouses are available in various materials from numerous sources, you may wish to build one yourself. Regarding layout and construction, consider the following diagram.

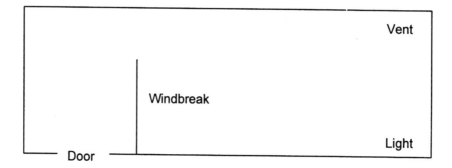

Face the *door* away from prevailing winds. The *windbreak*, which can be plywood, should extend from floor to ceiling and reach slightly more than halfway across the house's depth, to create a secure, dry, draft-free area for your pet. Discourage chewing by attaching heavy metal sheathing to the windbreak's exposed edge and the doorway. *Light* refers to a bulb of minimal but adequate wattage to provide heat. Install it in an unbreakable, waterproof (and dog-proof) fixture near the ceiling and shield all wiring in metal conduit. Place the *vent* near the ceiling also, using one of louvered design to repel moisture and promote drying.

Insulate the entire structure—walls, ceiling and floor—and raise it slightly above ground level to promote drying and avoid floor rot. In elevating the house, situate it such that pooch won't be able to move or tip it. The design should allow for only slightly more sleep space than the dog is large. We tend to transfer our own needs and wants to the building of a doghouse by making one too large and roomy. But dogs like small, secure nests, and too large a doghouse won't get used. Your pet must be able to easily turn around inside the rest area, but she needs no more room than that.

Slope the roof to promote water runoff. If the house is inside the run, make this angle slight so the dog can climb atop it to sun herself, as many dogs love to do. Finally, hinge the roof or make it detachable to facilitate cleaning.

For comfort's sake, cover the sleep area with wall-to-wall indoor/outdoor carpeting, surrounded with steel molding to discourage chewing of the edges. Don't just put cloth scraps in the doghouse—attach them. Otherwise, whatever you put in will be dragged out.

Alternatives to Doghouses

If your garage is heated, using a portion of it instead of a doghouse can affect overall cost. Though this may eliminate the need for a doghouse, you'll need an interior pen to confine your pet to one area. Attaching runs to a heated garage (or house or heated outbuilding) can be a sound move provided your dog can't escape into the garage or house, perhaps wreaking havoc on its contents and/or injuring herself. For security, and for times when you want to confine pooch to either her inside or outside run, the door to her outside-run area should be lockable. Also, keep five cautions in mind.

1. Make both the inside and outside enclosures four-sided, not three-sided. True, the wall of the building provides a fourth side, but it can also provide too much temptation for a chewer, especially a bored one confined in proximity to such material.
2. The building must have adequate interior drains for disposal of cleaning solutions.
3. If you use part of your garage for your pet's nest, the building must be well ventilated. Carbon monoxide and other vehicular emissions don't play favorites; they just kill.
4. If attaching to a garage, be certain your pet can't get at antifreeze—a tiny amount can be deadly.
5. Consider that in event of fire, pooch may be unable to flee far enough to avoid injury or death.

General Care and Comfort

In addition to the basic structures of the kennel, you should also provide some creature comforts for your dog:

- Safe chewables like Nylabones® can relieve your pet's boredom.
- A nearby radio playing gentle if not droning music can comfort a lonely dog. Avoid hard-rock or intense debate programming, as such racket can trigger anxiety.
- Blankets can afford a comfortable nesting area, but only if your pooch is not a chewer: Ingestion of clothlike materials can be fatal. Don't use straw or similar substances, because they can be an insect haven as well as a fire hazard.
- *Always* provide constant access to cool clean water, and be sure to place the dog's food and water bowls in a safe location. For example, don't place them near a fence that "outsiders" have access to; there's no reason to tempt ne'er-do-wells into harming your dog.

First-Aid Kit

If you don't already have a canine first-aid kit, get one. Keep it in an obvious location known to all adult family members. A complete kit's content is outlined in Chapter 5, "Equipment and Supplies," and a first-aid chart appears at the end of this book. Study it now, before you need to.

Record Keeping

Even though the kennel is for your own, personal use—as opposed to a profit-making venture—you should keep records pertaining to your kennel's initial construction cost as well as any improvements you make thereafter. If you sell your property, receipts and other paperwork relating to the kennel's construction could be useful when computing taxes.

Lest Ye Forget

A subtle effect of any kennel is that its availability can change the relationship between owner and dog, especially in the case of a housepet, and not always for the better.

The kennel is finished, all is in readiness and pooch is placed therein, "To try it out, you know." But over time she comes to spend more and more hours in the enclosure, though not by her choice. Kenneling, perhaps originally envisioned only for toilet purposes or when the family is away, becomes a habit. Banishment becomes routine, occasioned by such noteworthy events as company stopping by, or watching the big game, or the little game, or because it's Tuesday. Though the dog would surely rather be with what used to be her family, such closeness soon becomes a fading series of memories. The animal begins to find a hole in her life where her people used to be.

I tell you this because I've witnessed the phenomenon's subtle malignancy and distancing effects too often. From *Advanced Obedience Training—Easier Than You Think:* "Don't fall into the trap of allowing yourself to become so engrossed in training and competition that you forget why you ever got a dog in the first place." Excessive kenneling can foster a similar break, because then separation is physical as well as spiritual. By definition a kennel is a place for a dog, yes, but because pooch is your best buddy, better you view a kennel as an *occasional* place for a dog. Water-bucket heaters and self-feeders are all very well, but such gadgetry can lead to managing a pet's needs through automation rather than contact, as well as to keeping pooch from her family. If the weather can freeze a bucket of water, the message may be to let pupper share the warmth of the home. Excessive kenneling is jail time, nothing less, for crimes uncommitted.

Keep Reading

Pet owners should study both the home kennel and the boarding kennel sections as many conceptual similarities exist between boarding kennels and home kennels. Boarding-kennel concepts pertaining to design and construction can provide ideas you might adapt to your home-kennel needs.

*R*eflection

"Any place is good enough for a dog" is a venerable aphorism easy of quotation and capable of frequent application by those uninitiated in the management of dogs; but it is nevertheless wholly without foundation in fact, as those who have attempted to kennel valuable stock in unfitting quarters have discovered to their cost.

VERO SHAW, B.A. CANTAB.
THE ILLUSTRATED BOOK OF THE DOG
CASSELL AND COMPANY, LTD. (LONDON — 1880)

The Different Needs of Breeders and Trainers

Considerations for Breeders

Although this book is not about breeding, it does offer suggestions to help breeders establish a kennel or upgrade an existing
one. This section provides ideas about dam and puppy maintenance and welfare. In addition to reading this section, if you are
a breeder, you should also read the following portions of the
book because they provide information relevant for a breeding
kennel:

- The sections entitled "Choosing a Kennel Name—A Word
  on Marketing" and "Marketing Your Business," both in
  Chapter 4, "Setting Up Your Business"
- Chapter 1, "Designing and Building a Home Kennel," in
  its entirety
- Chapter 3, "Designing and Building a Boarding Kennel,"
  in its entirety
- Chapter 5, "Equipment and Supplies," in its entirety

Many breeding kennels are a combination of a home kennel and a boarding facility. They are generally somewhere in
between, in terms of the physical plant. Like a home kennel, the
breeding kennel houses the breeder's own pets. The difference
is in the objective: Birthing and caring for puppies, rather than
taking care of other people's dogs.

Placement and Provisions for the Maternity Ward

Breeders need more than just a kennel for housing young and mature dogs—they need a whelping area. Specifically, their dams need one. Granted, many healthy litters have been whelped in a guest-bedroom closet, but a professional breeder needs professional facilities.

Removed from noise and confusion—that's the first rule about siting a whelping area. Just as the guest-bedroom closet isn't ideal, neither is a kennel run. The whelping site should not be located anywhere in or even near a kennel—there's too much risk of disease transmission from other dogs. Locate your whelping area where you can control access and where day-to-day traffic is minimal. No, don't isolate the dam from her family—we don't want to ostracize her—but give her a secure, peaceful place. Barking dogs, ringing phones and doorbells, the presence of strangers and children running about at full yell don't make for a desirable whelping area. Such noises are not just distracting; they are disturbing and unsettling, and a dam can see them as threatening. Some very powerful drives (instincts) are going to be operating during the next few days and weeks, and while under normal conditions our pets flow with these occurrences, neither a dam nor puppies need stress.

The whelping area should be dry, well-ventilated yet draft-free, and easily cleaned. Its temperature should be as easily regulated as your home's. Make it small enough that the dam can feel secure—a large area can seem unsafe to a dog, as though there is too much room to defend—but not so small as to be cramped or stifling. The whelping room should have soft, clean bedding and cool, fresh water at all times. Keep rolls of paper towels on hand, as well as sanitized kitchen gloves (sterilized surgical gloves are even better) and various first-aid supplies (a complete list of first-aid items appears in chapter 5). Also, study a book covering emergency veterinary procedures pertaining to whelping, be thoroughly familiar with its contents, and keep your vet's phone number handy.

Those are musts. Niceties include an intercom for monitoring the whelping area without having to be there (many dams like uninterrupted periods of solitude), perhaps a radio tuned to a soft-music station, a pen and paper for recording noteworthy events, and a portable phone for contacting your vet without having to leave the dam.

Whelping Box

In your whelping area you need an open-top whelping box with sides high enough to provide emotional security for the dam and to contain the pups once they're old enough to move around. The box must be draft-free, as drafts can trigger a host of puppy illnesses. It can be made from plywood and should be large enough that the dam can stretch out at full length in any direction. Coat the box with lead-free paint, and raise it several inches above floor level to create a barrier against dampness. Prevent the dam from accidentally crushing or suffocating a puppy against a wall by installing guardrails three inches above, and parallel to, the floor on all four inside walls. I made my guardrails from one-inch by four-inch lumber cut to length and attached it to the sides using 90-degree angle braces. Create a U-shaped opening on one side of the box to allow the dam easy entrance and exit, but don't make the "U" so deep that puppies can get out of the box. Allowing for climate, place heat lamps a suitable height above the box to keep its inhabitants warm yet not overly so—your veterinarian can tell you the proper temperature to maintain. Don't use electric blankets or heating pads for warmth: If a dog chews one, she could be electrocuted. Do provide regular blankets, sheets, or large towels for the dam's comfort, however, and attach them to the floor in such a way that a puppy can't become entangled and suffocate.

Creating a Space for the Dam

Once you know the dam is indeed pregnant, take her to the site for brief familiarization visits. Ten minutes before the first pup arrives is not the time to introduce her to the whelping area. A day or so before the blessed event, move her into the whelping room for the duration. Remove her collar, lest Murphy's Law cause a puppy to become entangled and strangle. Continue to allow the dam periodic walks outside—she'll tell you when—but make the maternity ward her temporary home.

Privacy Considerations

Should children be allowed to observe puppies being born? It's difficult to formulate a blanket rule, as every child is an individual. Like adults, some have enough sense to deal with vital moments, whereas others do not. But since my primary concern during whelping is the dam and her offspring, I feel that it's best for her mental and emotional state to have only one or two adults she trusts on-hand. Moreover, it's inconsistent to infuse immaturity into a mature situation. We aren't staging a sideshow here, and the kids will have enough fun playing with the puppies in the weeks to come, as well they should: Children and puppies are made for each other. In the meantime, allow the dam an atmosphere of serenity and confidence. She deserves nothing less.

All Babies Are Beautiful

An experienced breeder can spot a "lesser than" puppy soon after one is born. A professional breeder knows that if any or all of a litter proves disappointing, such thoughts are best kept to oneself—don't express them around the dam. It isn't that she would necessarily understand your words but she knows your tones and she senses when you are displeased. She has done her best, and now you must do likewise by telling her how beautiful each puppy is, regardless of the truth of the situation.

Responsible Breeding

A perk to writing books is that you can express an opinion now and then that has absolutely nothing to do with the specific subject matter but everything to do with a more encompassing concern. (Of course, you have to hope your editor won't redline the section, but that's part of the game.)

First, consider that properly designed kennels, comfortable whelping areas and custom-printed pedigrees are all well and good, but for the sake of those puppies (and of dogs generally), please: Don't breed unless you are absolutely certain of finding homes for each puppy. And make that "*good* homes." The number of unwanted dogs destroyed annually at local shelters is sickening. If you are planning a litter, and if you know that a typical litter for your breed is *X* puppies, get at least that many responsible owners lined up before breeding. If you can't find that many people now, what makes you think you'll be able to once the pups are on the ground? I offer this advice to all breeders, but especially to those who own rarer, exotic breeds, as those puppies can be harder to place.

Point two: I mentioned "*good* homes." As defining such a home (a family, really) is difficult in terms of matching prospective buyers with a list of desirable attributes, it's one of those situations where you need to go with what your gut tells you. Follow the rule, "If in doubt, don't." Never let a pup go to a home you don't feel good about. Considerations such as a nice house in a good part of town, steady employment, regular churchgoers, 2.3 children and so on, are interesting facts, but they reveal absolutely nothing about character, compassion and a healthy sense of self-worth. When I visit with a prospective owner, it is for longer than just a few minutes; and though mine may seem a backward approach, I consciously look for reasons *not* to place a pup with the individual, not for reasons *to* place a pup. Reasons *to* will make themselves evident; reasons *not* to will be less apparent—the person will mask them—which is why I look for them in the first place.

Another gauge I rely upon comes from my adult dogs. They are friendly and outgoing, and if they don't feel good about an individual then that person doesn't get one of my pups, pure and simple. I have been told that this is overdoing it but each pup is counting on me to make the right choice, and since they are my pups I can do—or not do—anything I want with them without having to justify my decision or how I arrived at it. You have the same responsibility and the same freedom.

Paperwork and Transfer Practices

Just as a boarding-kennel operator follows procedures when releasing a pet to a client, you need practices pertaining to transferring a puppy to a new owner. The first is a bill of sale stating the pup's American Kennel Club or similar litter-registration number, her breed, gender, color, and markings and the names and ages and AKC or similar registration numbers of the sire and dam. The document should also include the whelping date and location, the breeder's name and address, the buyer's name and address, the date of sale and purchase price. Also, give the buyer the AKC or similar registration forms and a record of vaccinations the puppy has received and the dates when the next shots are due. A multigenerational pedigree is a thoughtful touch, as is a few days' supply of whatever food the puppy is accustomed to, and copies of any puppy photographs you may have taken and pictures of the parents. Buyers should also receive a copy of whatever contractual agreement the two of you have reached, copies of temperament-testing records you may have used, and a list of local veterinarians (assuming the buyer is from your locale.)

The actual transfer of the puppy should be accomplished over a period of at least an hour. Start the separation process by bringing the little one to an area that is well away from the litter. Encourage (through insistence, if need be) the buyer to spend some "get-acquainted" time with the pup before departing. For a puppy to leave the only home she has ever known is stressful, and a two-minute "Here's your pup; goodbye" transfer heightens that unrest. A gentle, gradual handing-over is not only much easier on the pup, it gives you a chance to get a final reading on the buyer. Have I ever called off a sale at this stage? No, but only because I have never felt that I needed to.

I also furnish buyers with a copy of my *Having To Do With Puppies*, a general "how-to" booklet on puppy raising and management. It is reprinted in the next section as a bonus, and although copies cannot be made of any portion of this book, you are welcome to retype, modify and distribute the *Having To Do With Puppies* material as you wish, provided you credit the source (*i.e.*, adapted from *Having To Do With Puppies*, from *Kennels & Kenneling* by Joel M. McMains, Howell Book House, New York, NY 2000).

Having To Do With Puppies

Feeding

Puppies attain 80 percent of their full growth within six to twelve months. In the process, they burn nearly double the daily calories, pound for pound, of mature dogs.

From weaning (around four weeks) until six months of age, feed the best puppy kibble (dry food) you can find. When first giving this solid food, stir in water to facilitate mastication and ingestion. Phase out this liquefying practice so that by seven or eight weeks of age, the food is completely dry.

Feed the pups four times daily—morning, noon, evening, bedtime—from weaning until they are ten to twelve weeks old, when you should eliminate the bedtime feeding. At five months, switch to morning and evening meals. This establishes the feeding pattern to follow throughout adult life. At about a year, switch to a maintenance-grade kibble during the warm months, and to one slightly higher in fat and protein for the cold seasons.

Though you should never remove a dog's bowl while he is in mid-bite, allow your pet only ten minutes or so to consume a meal. Then remove, wash and store the dish until the next scheduled feeding. Dogs are naturally fast eaters, hence the existence of expressions like "wolfing one's food." In the wild, a canine's natural setting, one eats as fast as possible, in case other animals covet the meal or circumstances cause its abandonment.

Avoid *on-demand* feeding, whereby food is always available. That can cause boredom, finicky eating habits and obesity. Of equal importance, it eliminates from the animal's emotional menu an opportunity for daily intimate contacts between dog and human, the essence of which has as much to do with bonding as with proper nutrition. Scheduled meals also let you know right away if your pet goes off his feed, which can signal illness.

Cool, Clear Water

Dogs of any age should have fresh water available during waking hours. Providing it in galvanized pails ensures they receive a daily trace of zinc, sometimes unavailable in commercial foods. Zinc is an important nutritional element, especially to breeds having erect to semi-erect ears as the chemical is thought to promote strong ear stance.

Snacks and Such

As far as when tidbits are appropriate and when they aren't, present a biscuit to your puppy when he arrives indoors after you have called him into the house. Rather than making this a constant practice, reward about three times out of four. That way, curiosity about whether there will be a tidbit can draw him to you. If a puppy learns a biscuit will always be offered, he may take it for granted and decide not to come just then.

Don't bribe. Don't stand by the door and wave the treat as you call pupper. Then you'd be offering him a choice whether to come, which is not a good idea at any age: Pooch could decide that he'd rather persist at whatever he's doing than stop for a snack. Get him inside, then present the morsel.

You may include small amounts of table scraps in scheduled feedings but not chicken bones and the like—they can be harmful, even deadly. Permissible between-meal snacks are dog biscuits in moderation.

Teething

A puppy begins to cut permanent teeth at around 16 weeks. Ease this uncomfortable time by providing rawhide chews, Nylabones® and the like. Gently massaging the young one's gums not only alleviates discomfort, but also strengthens the bond forming between you.

Housing and Housebreaking

A new puppy should sleep at your bedside in a properly sized, individual airline cage. This aids in housebreaking because a sound animal will not consistently foul his sleep area, provided you allow ample opportunity to seek relief at suitable locations. At bedtime, afford puppy a final evening walk, then take him straightaway to the cage.

While placing the pup in the enclosure, repeat the word "nest" several times, as this word best expresses the idea to communicate to the little one. The weekend is often a good time to acquaint puppy with the nest, as you may both lose some sleep that first night. To lessen undue worry and whining, place puppy treasures in the cage ahead of time— items such as a soft towel, maybe a ticking clock, possibly a Nylabone®, or perhaps an undershirt you wore that day (probably for the last time). But don't let any dog, young or old, shred a cloth article—ingestion of such material can kill.

A pup finding himself alone in a new situation may whine and fuss a bit, but after a time he'll usually settle. If he becomes unreasonably vocal, and if you're certain he isn't telling you that he *must* get outside (or is frightened), wiggling your fingers through the cage door and letting him lick them can do wonders. If the pup persists and begins to throw a snit, a squirt from a spray bottle filled with cold water can settle things. Accompany this with a curt but not roared "Out!", meaning "Not now," or more specifically in this case, "Hush." As the puppy calms, praise "Good Out."

Avoid moving the nest about the house. Part of its function is to create a sense of order and stability for a puppy, and periodic cage relocation can defeat this purpose. Similarly, don't let other pets or children enter or play with a pup's cage. The enclosure is something the young animal needs to think of as his, and his nose will tell him if he's had visitors.

The very first thing in the morning, you should take the puppy outdoors, repeating the cue "Yard" as you transport him there. If the nest is some distance from the door, prevent undesirable stops along the way by carrying him. Once he's back inside, keep your attention on him and be ready to take him outside speedily. Should you be occupied with some activity for a time—even just talking on the phone—put the puppy in his nest.

Remember that puppies initially have very little internal control. An active pup involved in play would rather continue what he's doing than stop to expel toxins. Thus, nature has constructed him in such a way that until he gains some maturity, he is simply unable to hold back the dam for more than a few seconds after his little brain issues the word. Once your pup gets "that look" in his eyes, you have very little time to get him outside.

The first time the puppy does goof in the house—and most pups do at least once—point his nose close to (but not into) the site of the transgression and repeat the word "No" in a firm, drawn-out manner. Don't speak harshly as that could frighten. More than one overly vocal owner has taught his pet through displays of righteous anger that the animal's natural urges were wrong. "Not here" is the message to communicate, not shame.

After drawing attention to the problem area, tote the puppy outside, encouragingly saying the word "Yard" as you proceed. Gathering up the accident and placing it at the location you want frequented can be helpful. The pup will find and sniff it, and will soon begin to get the idea.

As the young one performs his functions outside, praise (but softly, so as not to distract), saying, "Good piddle, good dump," or whatever phraseology you prefer. Later, during lengthy drives, telling your pet at a rest stop to "Go piddle" will often trigger the desired response.

During puppy's waking hours, regardless of whether he sends signals, make sure to take him outside every couple of hours. Also, walk him after naps, play sessions, meals and prolonged drinking. Those are times when puppies feel the need.

Unless you have no choice, avoid using newspapers for relief areas. "Paper training" is just that—it can teach a dog to respond to the feel of paper underfoot. Not only can a pup not differentiate between today's paper and the one you want him to use, he's being taught to use your house as a bathroom. True, the animal is standing on a newspaper, but he's still eliminating in your living space.

Exercise and Socialization

Exercise is as important to puppy well-being as proper nutrition. If a pup lacks either, healthy physiological or psychological development cannot occur. Your pet needs plenty of play space and lots of playtime with you.

Socialization entails taking a new puppy with you wherever and whenever circumstances permit. During life's first months, the number and quality of different situations, people and events a pup experiences can affect him for the rest of his days. Take your young dog to public parks, school areas or just for a drive, always keeping him on-leash. If you want your pet to be a member of your pack (family), treat him like one.

Never leave a dog unattended in a vehicle. The result can be chewed seats, a stolen pet or heatstroke. Heatstroke is often fatal and can occur quickly, even when outside temperatures are no warmer than 70 degrees.

Veterinarians

Like your family physician, your vet should be someone you have confidence in. (For information about locating a veterinarian, read the section "Choosing a Veterinarian" in Chapter 7, "Policies and Practices.") As a precautionary measure, any new puppy should be examined before or very soon after arriving at his new home.

Worms and Other Internal Parasites

Periodically take fecal samples to your vet for examination. If the tests are positive, treat the condition according to the doctor's instructions. Ask your DVM about heartworm preventive and the testing that precedes its initial use.

Shots and Vaccinations

After concluding puppy shots, have your pet vaccinated yearly against distemper, leptospirosis, hepatitis, parvovirus, rabies, coronavirus, and tracheobronchitis (kennel cough).

Medications

Giving pills and liquids are simple tasks made easier through conditioning during puppyhood. Give your pup placebos occasionally, always following such treatments with much praise and a dog biscuit. The treat not only lends a positive accent to the event, it makes sure the medication went down.

To give a pill, open the dog's mouth by reaching over the muzzle and inserting a fingertip directly behind a canine tooth (the longest upper tooth—there is one on each side). This causes nearly any dog to open his mouth. Holding the animal's nose upward, quickly but smoothly push the pill toward the back of the tongue. Withdraw your hand and gently hold the muzzle closed while softly stroking downward along the front of the throat.

Yes, you can be bitten during this procedure, but that's always the case when working around a dog's mouth.

To administer a liquid, first draw the fluid into a syringe. Then place the instrument's tip *without* a needle attached) in the fold of your pet's cheek near the back teeth while using minimal pressure to hold the muzzle barely closed. Don't push the plunger so fast that your dog inhales the liquid rather than swallowing it.

Grooming

Dogs usually shed two or three times yearly. Gently brush your pup twice a week. Bathe him as needed but not more than six times a year, lest you dry the skin and coat. Trim nails and clean ears weekly. Since there are breed differences about performing these chores, ask your vet or breeder to show you appropriate procedures.

Training

While formal obedience is generally best deferred until the sixth month, you can lay much groundwork during puppyhood. This is especially true in terms of bonding and attitude building.

Precisely when to start formal training depends upon the animal's temperament and maturity and the trainer's abilities and experience. Starting too soon can do more harm than good since a puppy who experiences fright during a critical developmental period, whether it be of a collar, a leash or—God forbid—of you, will never outgrow the feeling, regardless of ensuing positive learning experiences. In the Howell book *The New Knowledge of Dog Behavior*, Clarence Pfaffenberger quotes J. Paul Scott, Ph.D.:

It is important to remember that, while previous learning may be altered by subsequent learning, subsequent learning will never obliterate previous learning.†

Until you discern some maturation in the young one, such as a lengthened attention span, let the puppy be a puppy.

In other words, if in doubt, don't.

Puppy Obedience Classes

I have mixed feelings about the concept of puppy obedience classes. They are fine as a socialization vehicle, but that potential is offset by their inherent risk for spreading disease. It takes time for a young immune system to develop, and some breeds are more susceptible to disease than others.

From a training standpoint, puppy classes can easily be detrimental. For instance, in many classes a puppy is taught he may ignore or respond to his owner's command to Sit (for example), as no meaningful force is used to back up the command. The problem is that "Sit" does not mean, "Smack your butt onto the ground, then hop up and do whatever you please," though without enforcement that is how a pup typically responds, especially among peers.

A professed puppy class goal is to demonstrate obedience is a fun and pleasant activity. This sounds good on paper, but two problems exist. First, this positive attitude should be a constant: It should operate in any training program, regardless of the animal's age. Second, while it's true that no puppy should be pressured—inappropriate force can scare him at a time when he's highly vulnerable—it's equally true that no dog should ever be taught that a command allows a choice on his part, especially during the impressionable phase of puppyhood.

Puppy class supporters promote the view that the "You must!" aspect of obedience is added to the program when pooch is old enough to handle it. That's a mixed signal, which is my objection; to initially demonstrate that commands are open to a vote and then later change the rules can instill confusion and distrust in any animal.

Unintended Lessons

Consider the following example of subtle, inadvertent training. Should a sudden sound cause puppy to startle, ignore both the noise and his

---

† J. Paul Scott, Ph.D., as quoted by Clarence Pfaffenberger in *The New Knowledge of Dog Behavior* (New York: Howell Book House, Inc., 1963), p. 132. This book is an excellent source for further information about critical periods.

anxiety. Rushing to him with, "It's all right. Don't worry," and so forth, may only reinforce his nervousness to sudden noises. Yes, pet him as you normally would if he comes to you, but no, don't fly to pupper to reassure. Sound dogs have no built-in fear of thunder—it's a natural phenomenon and dogs are beings of nature—but many owners unwittingly educate their pets to fear loud noises. While reassurance can be helpful with some children, it's a sure way to cause apprehension and anxiety in a dog. His reaction to pointless reassurance is, "If everything's so fine and dandy then just what are *you* so concerned about?" If a given sound doesn't worry you, don't teach your pet to fear it.

You're Always on Stage

Similarly, remember that whenever you are near your companion, even if you're not actively engaged with him, you are in fact teaching him, whether you mean to or not. Be aware, and be careful.

Collars

Regardless of the type of collar you prefer, remove it from your pet's neck when you aren't going to be nearby for a while—even for a few minutes! A curious and adventuresome puppy can discover myriad ways of catching a collar on something. Such happenings are usually traumatic and can easily be fatal.

The Playtoy

Play with your puppy using tennis balls, laundered burlap sacks, Frisbees™—whatever seems to turn him on. Regardless of your toy selection, don't leave the special playtoy lying around where the pup can see it, lest the article lose its attraction. If the toy is always present, a pup can easily learn to take it for granted. It is to appear only when you do, and then only sometimes. The idea is for the pup to learn to associate the pleasurable object with you.

The few rules governing the proper use of play articles come under the heading of, "A Puppy Cannot Do Anything Wrong with a Playtoy." That is, if he is interested in the thrown ball, fine. Should he give chase and pounce upon it, fine. If he picks it up and runs away from you with it, fine. If he goes to the bathroom on it, fine. He cannot do anything improper with a playtoy—that's just not possible. Sending any negative messages that a puppy could relate to the play item can easily lessen his attraction to it.

To instill and heighten puppy's interest in a toy, begin by kneeling next to him. (The dominating pressure imparted by body language when standing over a young animal can distract from the moment—in general, things above a dog seize his attention.) Roll the ball back and forth, staring pointedly at the object while observing the pup's reactions peripherally. As interest develops, move the article behind your leg, to cause him to look for the toy. As puppy fascination increases, allow him to pounce upon and carry off the object to the accompaniment of your voiced approval.

The objective is to tempt the puppy with a toy until he displays strong attraction to it. If it's easy for the pup to capture the article, he can lose interest in it because it lacks challenge and stimulation. At the same time, don't prolong the teasing to an extent that desire wanes. That could teach a pup a losing attitude.

When playing with very young or inexperienced animals, roll a ball for them rather than throwing it. Until a young dog has had some practice in pursuing an object, he is unable to follow the flight of a thrown ball with his eyes and can easily become confused or frustrated to the extent of losing interest. Field and depth of vision expand with maturity.†

If you're working with several puppies, just dropping a playtoy in their vicinity entices them. One pup will grab the object, if for no other reason than to prevent another from doing so, and the game has begun. If you have an older dog who enjoys chasing a ball, allow the pups to watch from a safe distance, preferably from behind a fence so they cannot interfere and perhaps be snapped at. The idea is to stimulate interest and heighten the desire to participate.

Praise

When your puppy does something that pleases you, tell him. For example, when he trots back to you with *his* ball, pet and praise the young one, saying, "Good Bring." Don't be in a hurry to take the object from him, lest he learn to come with lowered head or not to come at all. When you do take the article, immediately throw or roll it again. Don't tease excessively first: Take the toy, wave it in front of pupper's nose a time or two and throw it. Dogs enjoy pursuit as much as they do possession. We want to show your pet that it's in his interest to release the toy to you, and then to keep his eyes on you.

Pet a puppy, especially one with erect ears, under the chin and along the underside of the neck and muzzle. The idea is to teach your pet to look up at you. It's especially important for outsiders to whom you grant

---

† Canines are born nearsighted. This is a survival mechanism since puppies could otherwise be drawn from the protection of the nest toward injurious or life-threatening situations.

petting privileges to use this manner of touching. Petting a dog atop the head can cause him to lower it while pulling his ears down submissively, and it is unwise to suggest a mind-set of automatic submission toward strangers. Friendliness and curiosity, yes, but submission, no.

Identifiers and Language

Facilitate communication by assigning names to things for your puppy. In addition to their command vocabularies, my dogs have an understanding of objects and concepts numbering another 40-odd terms. Some handy words are: *outside, yard, car, truck, house, chair, couch, bed, nest,* (food) *dish, dinner* (feeding time), *drink, ball, leash, collar, sack* (burlap), *rabbit, kitty, horse, bird, critter* (bovine), *deer, warm,* and *cold.*

Protection

Take precautions for your pup's well-being and safety. One is an area securely fenced to a minimum height of five feet. That may seem excessive if yours is a small dog, but keep in mind that while a fence is intended to contain your pal, it is also to keep intruders out. There are those disposed to taking things that do not belong to them, your pet included.

Two other safeguards are a watchful eye and no patience with anyone who attempts to tease your pet. Dogs possessing even minimum intelligence and spirit seldom tolerate such abuse for long, and they shouldn't have to.

Don't tie a dog. The practice can easily induce paranoia and an aggressive attitude since the animal's primary defense, the ability to run away, has been taken from her. Tying can create distrust toward yourself, too, as it is you who have taken away the possibility of escape.

Discourage the behavior of cretinous types who seem compelled to act in an agitating or teasing manner when finding themselves near a Doberman, German Shepherd, Rottweiler or any large dog. Similarly, waste no patience on the clown who habitually ridicules smaller members of the canine world. Such a person's frail ego may need the stimulation, but pooch's spirit is your first concern.

On a related theme, I never take my dogs off-leash to a public area, regardless of their age or depth of training. I don't ever want to find myself in a courtroom, trying to phrase a disarming reply to the learned judge's query, "Has the dog been trained to bite?" The fact that a child was nipped while trying to stick the animal in the eye may prove a shallow defense. Irrespective of whether your dog is ever guard trained, keep him on-leash whenever you two are out in public, lest some yahoo wind up owning your house.

In Closing

The following is adapted from the *Ten Commandments* of the software program *Canis*, and are used with permission from Centron Software Technologies, Inc.

1. My life is likely to last 10 to 15 years. Any separation from you will be painful for me. Remember that before you buy me.
2. Give me time to understand what you want of me.
3. Place your trust in me—it's crucial to my well-being.
4. Don't be angry at me for long, and don't lock me up as punishment. You have your work, your entertainment, and your friends. I have only you.
5. Talk to me sometimes. Even if I don't understand your words, I understand your voice when it's speaking to me.
6. Be aware that however you treat me I'll never forget it.
7. Remember before you hit me that I have teeth that could easily crush the bones of your hand but that I choose not to bite you.
8. Before you scold me for being uncooperative, obstinate, or lazy, ask yourself if something might be bothering me. Perhaps I'm not getting the right food, or I've been out in the sun too long, or my heart is getting old and weak.
9. Take care of me when I get old; you too will grow old.
10. Go with me on difficult journeys. Never say, "I can't bear to watch it," or, "Let it happen in my absence." Everything is easier for me if you are there. Remember, I love you.

Should You Consider Boarding?

Even if you periodically have room to handle boarders for some extra income, think twice before bringing strange dogs into your kennel. New dogs in the area are stressful to those already in residence, and there's always the chance of someone's pet bringing diseases to your facility. Understand: I'm not saying that boarding is out of the question for breeders; I'm suggesting that the costs of boarding can be higher than one might suspect.

Considerations for Trainers

Training facilities are generally akin to boarding kennels in terms of physical layout and responsibilities. The biggest difference is purpose: Instead of just maintaining someone's pet for a few days, training kennels board for extended periods and train dogs as well. Accordingly, trainers should read all of Section II, "Boarding Kennels," which consists of chapters 3 through 10.

Equipment Storage

When designing your storeroom, allow ample room for equipment. I'm not referring to jumps, scaling walls and the like—such large items can be kept outdoors—but to leashes, collars, dumbbells and protection gear (assuming you train guard dogs), such as body suits and padded sleeves.

The Training Yard

A main consideration when planning a training kennel is room for, and location of, a training area. If you have limited real estate, locate the kennels so that one large section of land is left for training purposes, rather than configuring the overall layout so that two or three small areas of land are available as training yards. Simply put, one large area measuring at least 100 feet on each side affords more flexibility than do several small yards.

Surround the training yard with a high fence (six to eight feet) that cannot be climbed. For security, keep gates locked when the area is not in use. There should be shade from a few shade trees in or adjacent to the site, and if you plan to do night training, install exterior lighting in at least one area of the yard.

Whether the training yard should be visible from the kennels is an important consideration. Some trainers feel that dogs learn better by watching others being worked. Others say this knocks down the spirits of dogs temporarily "left behind" while others are being trained. My view is that the audience effect is beneficial for all concerned, especially in terms of motivation: The animal being trained is "on stage," getting an opportunity to show the others how it should be done, and the dogs observing are getting psyched up for their chance to perform.

If you prefer to isolate your training yard from the kennel, an obvious solution is to erect a wooden fence. The drawback to such a fence, of course, is that it must be painted or stained periodically, and it can be chewed and may be easy to climb.

Do you teach obedience classes and the like in your training yard? If so, hang a sign at the entrance: "Dog Training Area—Enter at Your Own Risk." Posting such a warning may not afford a great deal of legal protection but, as an attorney told me, "You may be safer with it than without it."

A large training area adjacent to the kennels.

Also, presuming that you do not allow smoking in your training area (I don't), hang a small bucket containing a few inches of water near your gate but above curious-dog level and advise smokers, "Put 'em out in the bucket." If you don't provide such a receptacle, cigarettes will merely be dropped and ground out on your lawn, which can lead to muttered imprecations the first time your mower chews up a filtered butt.

Forms and Records

Many of the forms presented in Section II, "Boarding Kennels," can be adapted to training kennel use. A case in point is the following Training Record and Training Contract for use with dogs boarded with you for on-leash obedience training. I print the Training Record and the Training Contract on opposite sides of the same piece of paper to centralize records and reduce waste. If you use separate forms, add a line to the Training Contract showing the owner's name—signatures are not always legible.

As you will see, the primary difference between the Training Contract form and its cousin presented in the "Boarding Kennels" section is the wording. The Training Contract details the training the dog is to

Kennel Name
City and State
Training Record

Owner	Dog's Call Name

Address	Breed

at

City, State, Zip	Age	Date	Sex	Alt

Telephone	E-mail	Veterinarian

Medical Problems, Allergies, etc.

Vaccinations: ☐ Rabies ☐ Distemper ☐ Parvo-Virus
☐ Corona ☐ Kennel Cough ☐ Other: _____

Food: Kennel's _____   Amount per Feeding (cups):
AM ____   N ____   PM ____   E ____
Owner's _____

IN Date/Time	OUT Date/Time	Collar	Leash	Bed	Food	Med	Other	Charges

Training Notes: _____

_____

_____

_____

_____

_____

_____

_____

Kennel Name

Address

City, State, Zip Code

TRAINING CONTRACT

This is a Contract between [*Kennel Name*] and the pet Owner.

Kennel agrees to exercise due and reasonable care, and to keep the kennel premises sanitary and properly enclosed. The dog(s) is to be fed properly and regularly, and to be housed in clean, safe quarters.

All dogs are boarded or are otherwise handled or cared for by Kennels without liability on Kennel's part for loss or damage from disease, theft, fire, death, running away, injury, or harm to persons, other dogs, or property by said dog, or other unavoidable causes, due diligence and care having been exercised.

Obedience training will cover on-leash commands to sit, heel, sit automatically during heeling when the handler stops moving, lie down, come when called, and jump over an obstacle. Play-type retrieving will be taught to those dogs who, in the Kennel's sole judgment, show a pronounced instinct for such activity. Owner agrees to pay to Kennel [*fee, in numbers*] ([*fee, in words*]) per pet for such training.

All charges incurred by Owner shall be payable upon pickup of pet(s). Owner further agrees that pet(s) shall not leave the Kennels until all charges are paid to Kennel by Owner. Owners of pet(s) left at the Kennels beyond the agreed pick-up date will be charged for boarding pet(s)at a rate of [*rate, in numbers*] ([*rate, in words*]) per day until pet(s) is claimed.

Kennel shall have, and is hereby granted, a lien on the pet(s) for any and all unpaid charges resulting from boarding and/or training pet(s) at Kennel.

If the pet(s) becomes ill or if the state of the animal's health otherwise requires professional attention, Kennel, in its sole discretion, may engage the services of a veterinarian of its choosing, or administer medicine, or give other requisite attention to the animal, and the expenses thereof shall be paid by Owner.

It is understood by Kennel and Owner that all provisions of this Contract shall be binding upon both parties thereunto for this visit and for all subsequent visits.

This Contract contains the entire agreement between the parties.

_____	_____
Owner	*Date*
_____	_____
Kennel	*Date*

receive, and states that owners who leave animals beyond the scheduled departure date will be charged at your current boarding rate.

Owner Visitation Rights During Training

Owners sometimes ask to visit their pet while he is with me for training. While some trainers have no problem with such a request, my practice is summarized in the phrase, "No way!" (Of course, I explain my policy's rationale to owners in more diplomatic fashion.) An owner showing up for a few hours now and then not only disrupts my day generally and my training schedule specifically, but is hard on the dog: The animal can't understand why he has to stay behind when the owner leaves. It is difficult enough to get an animal settled for the demands of training without periodic appearances by members of the dog's family. The effect of such visits, which make more sense in people terms than in dog terms, can be to distract the dog for several days after the fact.

Graduation from Training—The Big Day

Just as this book is not about breeding, neither is it a training manual. Still, I would be ducking an issue were I not to outline general procedures relating to dealing with owners, especially in terms of turning over a trained dog to an excited client.

An owner has arrived to collect his pet. You have spent some time visiting with the individual, detailing his dog's training, summarizing how the animal has fared, discussing certain training basics. Today is the day; pooch is going home. But don't let the dog know that. Not yet, anyway.

My practice, after meeting with the owner, is to leave the individual at a place where he can see the training yard but which is downwind and some distance from it. I then go leash up pooch, and work the animal as the owner looks on. I caution the client ahead of time to make no sounds or movements that might catch the dog's attention. I then bring the animal to the owner and for the next few minutes, as I earlier told the person would be the case, all bets are off. Sure, the dog could be made to hold a sit-stay, for instance, while the owner greets the dog, but that isn't obedience, it's cruelty. If the dog is a large animal I'm not going to let him knock his owner flat, but at the same time I won't thwart reasonable displays of joy and affection. The length of time of the reuniting process varies from owner to owner, but you should count on spending at least a couple of hours with the client from the time he arrives to get the dog.

After a few minutes I hand the owner the leash and tell him something like, "Here are the keys. Now let's see you work your dog." My role then becomes one of teacher while I watch the team go through various paces. As the objective is not to turn the owner into a trainer but a handler of a trained dog, once it is apparent that the individual has a few basic concepts in mind and seems at ease working his dog, it is time they were on their way. A person can only absorb so many new ideas in a given period of time, and the dog can only be worked for so long without becoming tired or bored.

To help the owner along in acquiring training skills and concepts, I present him with a copy of the following list of training basics (which, like the *Having To Do With Puppies* booklet, you are welcome to retype and distribute as you wish, provided you credit this book and its publisher as the source).

Some Training Hints

The key to effective training is establishing communication based on bonding. Said another way, whatever feelings and attitudes you send down the leash will come back to you. That's the overall concept. Following are bits and pieces I hope you'll find useful.

- Don't work your dog sooner than an hour after feeding her, and give her ample opportunity to relieve herself before work or play begins. If you work your pet for 15 minutes a day, play with her for 15 minutes a day, but keep playtime separate from work for now. Have pooch wear the training collar during both activities, but give no commands during play periods. Put the play object away from her sight after play. If the toy is left to lie around, it loses its magic. Play objects that you may later wish to use in teaching other work should not be used as distractions. Some good distractions are other animals, people and traffic settings.
- Teach new lessons in distraction-free areas, adding distractions gradually and only after learning has occurred. Family members may be present, but they shouldn't say the dog's name or make eye contact with her. Give *one* clear command and proceed. Use commands only when you mean to, and don't give commands you can't immediately enforce physically. Avoid using the dog's name with commands; use it sometimes during praise; *never* use it during correction. Don't train when you are tired, ill, pressed for time or irritated, and don't prolong any exercise to the extent that you guarantee your pet a correction. That teaches a dog to lose.
- Praise according to what your dog has just done, like "Good Sit," "Good Bring" and so on, not "Good girl," "Good dog" etc. Don't

loom over your pet when praising her and don't pound on her in affection. Pet calmly and speak quietly, sending approval rather than affection. A dog should be given affection throughout her life—she shouldn't have to work for it. Similarly, anger has no place in correction. The dog's behavior is what's at issue, not the worth of the dog herself.

- Vary your sessions' times and locations, working indoors as well as out and in all reasonable forms of weather. End each period on a positive note, with the dog having just done an exercise right and been praised. Don't involve your pet in any other activity (including feeding) immediately after training. Let her have some quiet time.
- For now your dog should have only one trainer—you.
- Smokers should avoid their habit during training/play sessions.
- Don't tolerate improper aggression from your dog, ever.
- *Never allow an unsupervised dog to wear any collar! Should the animal accidentally hook the collar on something, he could strangle to death.*

Should You Consider Boarding?

You might want to consider offering boarding services in addition to training. If you have the time and interest to do it properly, my thought is, "Why not?" You can garner extra income and you may convince some owners to have you train their pets. Just remember that boarding takes time, and that no dog should be neglected for other activities, like training.

Realize also that boarding can lower your income. Suppose you have a full kennel and someone calls about training. You'd like to take the dog right away, but a boarder has the run you need and she's scheduled to be there for several weeks. If the caller decides against waiting and contacts another trainer, that's lost money because you make much more from training a dog than boarding one.

Professional Considerations

Although this book does not address professional training per se, record keeping is still a must. To that end, photograph each dog from several angles upon arrival and just before departure. Include in each shot an assistant as a witness and the current day's newspaper in the foreground, to show the date. Note in the dog's file any injury or disabilities. Should an unethical owner claim you allowed the dog to rip up her footpads, for example, you want evidence that the animal left your kennels in as good or better shape than when she arrived.

You may wonder if I have encountered such ruthlessness. I have. Once. That was enough. The photographs, which the owner did not know existed, along with witness corroboration, saved the day, though the phrase "countersuit" helped also.

During training sessions I carry a pocket cassette recorder for making on-site notes, which I later transcribe into each dog's training file. Although you may be able to keep in your head all necessary details about each dog's progress, if you're ever hauled into court about one you trained, written records may prove persuasive to a jury. That you maintain documentation can also accent your professionalism, certainly more than would a scratch of the head and comments that begin, "Well, as I recollect . . . ."

Once each dog's training is complete, videotape a session showing all elements of the animal's schooling. Make a copy for the owner and keep one yourself. Include audio on the tape so commands can be heard, attesting that you didn't have to cue the dog repeatedly to elicit proper responses.

Not incidentally, I don't charge extra for providing owners a copy of their pets' video tapes. Owners doubtless play them for friends, which generates referrals for me.

Groom the dog before her departure. Despite your kennel's cleanliness, dogs confined for extended periods can take on a "kennel smell." Don't let this condition scar your training efforts.

A few days after the dog departs, contact the owner and ask how pooch is doing. No, you're not worried—don't send that message—you're just interested. Should an owner wish to bring the dog out for brief brush-up work, not as a boarder but just to spend some time in your training yard, don't charge for it. Goodwill is more valuable.

Reflection

Every dog is a lion at home.

TORRIANO, *PIAZZA UNIVERSALE*, 36 (1666)

Boarding Kennels

3

Designing and Building a Boarding Kennel

My toughest planning question was, "Which question do I deal with first?" When considering all the variables—size of operation, location, overall layout, the building's design, heating, cooling, plumbing and waste-disposal systems, electrical wiring, security fencing, landscaping—and the variations of every variable, the list of choices can seem endless and overwhelming.

Consider a few questions about something as basic as outdoor runs. What surface is best: gravel, dirt, concrete or some other material? How many runs should I have? What direction should they face with regard to sunlight and weather? What size should they be? Should they all be the same size? Should I use fencing or some other material to separate each run? If fencing, what type is best? Chainlink? Woven wire? Non-climb? Something else? Should I fence the tops of the runs?

As you see, a great many important decisions await you. This chapter will help you determine the questions you need to answer, and to offer options and planning techniques.

Planning the Project
Building Permits and Zoning Restrictions

The first step in the planning process is to consult the "powers that be" in charge of issuing building permits and the like, and determine whom you will have to keep happy about what. If you are fortunate enough to live on what is generally termed "unrestricted land," you may be in for a much easier time than if your area has a proliferation of building regulations, zoning restrictions and covenants, and is controlled by herds of bureaucrats. Regardless of what you *think* you know about your locale's land laws, find out for sure what you're up against and how to satisfy the system.

A related consideration regards readers who are looking for property on which to build a home and a kennel. Unless you plan to have an in-town kennel in a locale where it's legal to do so, seek at least a semi-isolated setting. Perhaps you'll find a location near a residential area where establishing a kennel is legal. Though no restrictions may exist that would hamper your project, it would be wiser, as well as more considerate, to seek a more remote area. Perhaps you would not be violating any laws or regulations by building your kennel in or near a populated area, but you might well incur sufficient ill will from local citizenry to harm your business.

Once your structure is built, what local ordinances pertaining to inspections and certifications have to be completed before you can do business? If you don't know, find out, and make sure your facility is in compliance.

Overall Size of Kennel

This is a candle-and-flame type of decision, as the size is invariably dependent upon the location. There's no point in planning a 30-run facility if you only have room for 10. My steps for answering "What size?" begin by determining the size of a single outdoor run. Since outdoor runs require more area than indoor ones, they are a primary consideration in allotment of space.

1. To afford adequate exercise room for a large dog, what size should your outside runs be? Mine are 16 feet long by 4 feet wide. These dimensions may seem restrictive for housing an Irish Wolfhound, for example, but remember that the nature of a boarding kennel is to house occupants temporarily, not permanently. Breeders of large dogs need larger runs. Also, consider that should you have to deal with an aggressive animal, there is a thin line between limiting how much of a rush you want her to be able to take at you and having adequate maneuvering room for yourself. Of course, if you plan to board only small dogs, runs 16 feet long by 4 feet wide may be about 8 feet too long and a foot too wide.

2. Should all outdoor runs be the same size? One school of thought recommends constructing runs of two basic sizes, the rationale

being that seldom will the kennels be filled totally by large dogs. Since a percentage of the runs will often be occupied by small animals, why not save on construction costs by making some of the runs small?

While that argument has merit, my preference is to have all large runs. True, I rarely have a kennel full of big dogs, but it does happen. By limiting the size of some of my runs I am limiting the number of large dogs I can *properly* house. Yes, a Newfoundland will survive a few days of being boarded in a small run, but that isn't the point. That Newf or any other dog is entitled to the same degree of comfort as the Papillon boarded next to her, which the sardine effect of too much dog in too little space does not provide.

3. Once you have determined the size of your outside runs, decide how many your kennel should have. The first factor in this equation is the size of your property: Does it limit the number of runs your facility can have? If so, how many runs do you have room for? Note this number, mark it "Space for" and set it aside a moment.

4. If space imposes no restrictions, how many runs can you service daily? Assuming a maximum occupancy of two dogs per run (both owned by the same person, of course), how many runs can you effectively deal with? Write down this number, mark it "Serviceable runs" and set it aside.

5. Which number is less, "Space for" or "Serviceable runs"? Tentatively, that's the number of runs your kennel should have. If you have room for, say, 30 runs, but you sense that you don't have the time to deal properly with more than 20 runs daily, 20 is the number to hang onto for the moment. Mark this number "Tentative." We'll come back to it.

6. This last consideration can be the trickiest variable in the formula. Answer the question, "How many runs do you think you could rent on an average day once your business has built up a clientele, a following?" If you have difficulty pinning down a number, visit with other local dog folk (groomers, breeders, trainers, but *not* other boarding-kennel operators, for obvious reasons) and put the question to them, asking them to respond as though they were planning a boarding kennel. Talk with enough people who are sincere in giving you their best estimates, and in time you will start to notice a commonality among their responses. Why? Because they are local dog folk, and as such they have a feel for the needs in your locale. They have a sense, an awareness, of the potential, even if they have never pondered the question. Once you have concluded your

informal survey, the likelihood is that the number mentioned most often will be very close to the one you had settled on, perhaps without even realizing you had. It will sound right to you.

In any case, let's say that number is 12. Your gut feeling, and that of your friends, is that once your enterprise gets rolling, you will be able to fill a dozen runs on an average day. Now multiply that number by 2. Remember, we are asking how many runs you could sell on an *average* day. Some days you will have fewer runs occupied, some days more, and my experience is that I fill about twice as many runs during peak periods than during average days. Hence, the multiplier factor of 2, which in this example leads us to a need for 24 runs. Note that number and mark it "Peak demand."

Is this a foolproof formula for projecting demand, a product of cold analytical study, resplendent in such phraseology as "demographic analysis" and "computer modeling"? Hardly. Some might feel that it's laughable. But it's rooted in the simple fact that without spending a small fortune on professional surveys and the like, you have to go with your reading of your area to answer the question, "How many runs can I fill daily once my business is established?" This estimate can best be enhanced by the opinions of other area dog people who are likely to have a good feel for the demand where they live. Then double that number to lessen the incidence of turndowns during busy times.

7. Compare that last number, which you labeled "Peak demand," with the one you earlier marked "Tentative;" the lower number is the number of runs you should construct. If the "Peak demand" number is 24, but the "Tentative" number is only 20, plan your kennels on the basis of having 20 runs. True, we have concluded that you could fill 4 more runs during high-demand times of the year, but 20 runs are all you feel you can handle. Had our "What can we sell daily?" analysis resulted in 7 runs, for instance, we would plan on the facility having 14 runs (7 times 2). You can handle 20 runs a day, yes, but the market will only support 14 at best, so there is no point in constructing the extra 6 runs.

Consider one final factor pertaining to run count. Let's say that our analysis fixes 14 runs as your optimal number. Round that figure to 15. Why? Because many commercial suppliers of chainlink kennels—which is the best material for the money for a boarding kennel—routinely prefabricate run gates in banks of five. The per-item cost difference of prefabricated gate panels versus that of individual gates can be significant, enough to absorb the cost of constructing a 15th run even though you determined that 15 runs was the optimal number. Remember, too, that our calculations of "How many runs should I build?" is seat-of-the-pants in nature, and a margin of error of plus-or-minus 1 or 2 runs is acceptable.

In each section, when comparing two numbers pertaining to how many runs to build, I have recommended choosing the lower number. This comes from my err-on-the-side-of-caution tendency in dealing with dog-related issues, from how firmly to initiate discipline to how many runs to erect. Just as a trainer can always get firmer with a dog should the need arise, design your kennel such that there is little risk of overbuilding but in such a way that you can expand it.

The cautious approach can seem tedious and unexciting at times, but consider that if you do expand later, after results have demonstrated that demand is greater than supply, you'll be in a position to add-on by using other people's (clients') money; additions will be paid for from profits, not from your original capital.

Don't Restrict Yourself from Future Expansion

Even if you don't ever envision expanding the kennels, don't restrict today what you might change your mind about tomorrow. True, a kennel having a certain number of runs may be as large as you will ever want to operate, but what if someday you decide to sell out? Suppose a buyer would meet your price except that he wants to increase the number of runs and sees that the design of your kennel would make it cost-prohibitive to do so. Or suppose that someday you decide to add sales of equipment or food to your operation. Is your planned storeroom large enough to handle an inventory of such items? Those are but two reasons why it is better not to limit tomorrow's options today.

The Bottom Line for Planning

The point of all this is that when planning a major installation like a boarding kennel, you need to get it as right as possible the first time. "Should," "probably," "maybe," "good enough" and "that might work" are words and phrases that have no place in the planning, design or construction of a kennel, any more than they do in the designing and building of a house. True, many design faults can be corrected after construction, but it's far less stressful on the pocketbook (and on you) to get it right from the start.

Designing the Kennel
Configuration

How do you envision the overall layout of your kennel? Will it have runs on only one side of the building? On two sides? Three? Four? Concepts to factor into your decision are *centralization, best use of available space, security*, and *weather*, though not necessarily in that order.

What is meant by *centralization*? Consider an extreme example of noncentralization: a four-run kennel having one run on each of the building's four sides. Sure, that's a ludicrous configuration, but it illustrates the principle of centralization. Runs scattered about a building are impractical, if for no other reason than that you'd spend too much time going from run to run just to clean them. Properly centralized, the four runs would be adjacent to each other on one side of the building. This would facilitate quick cleaning, as you could go directly from one run to the next.

Best use of available space is akin to the centralization concept, although the two can be at odds with one another. Visualize a 10-run kennel having all runs on one side of the building. That's a centralized configuration, but it may not represent the best use of available space: Three sides of the building are unused. Such a layout may be appropriate in some situations, as when the kennel building serves more than one purpose and the other sides are better used for other functions. When discussing a structure that is intended solely as a boarding kennel, however, it's preferable to use the entire building. Accordingly, were I designing a 10-run facility, I would locate five runs on each of two opposite sides and would place a storeroom on one end and leave the other wall open for access and for possible future expansion.

A principle as important as the *best use of available space* and *centralization* concepts is *security*. Security refers to such notions as having multiple exterior doors for fire-escape purposes. Installing locks on those doors, erecting a perimeter fence around the kennel area, and locating the facility so that all outdoor runs are visible from your house are other examples of *security*, as are run gates that can be padlocked, a fence around your property (in addition to the perimeter fence surrounding the kennel), a motion sensor in the storeroom, and smoke detectors and charged fire extinguishers throughout the building. Other security measures include installing all electrical outlets and switches higher than most dogs can reach and surrounding the kennel building with wide walkways of shale, gravel or a similar substance that is noisy when trod upon, making it difficult if not impossible for an intruder to approach the facility without alerting its occupants (whose barking would alert you).

Finally, consider *weather*. Runs should be sited so that none continually takes the brunt of summer heat or prevailing winter winds. Yes, all runs should receive some daily sunshine—sunlight is an excellent disinfectant—but no run should be exposed to perpetual, cook-an-egg-on-its-surface heat. Does this mean that south-facing runs cannot be erected? No. It means that runs can be pointed in any direction you want, provided you install sunscreens, erect windbreaks and/or have trees for shade and protection from winter's blasts.

Even allowing for the foregoing constraints, overall kennel configuration is limited only by your imagination. Following is a rough floor plan for a 10-run facility. It is not presented as being inherently better or more complete than one you might come up with. It is simply a possibility, offered to give you ideas.

		Door			
Outdoor Run #1	1		6	Outdoor Run #6
Outdoor Run #2	2	L	7	Outdoor Run #7
Outdoor Run #3	3		8	Outdoor Run #8
Outdoor Run #4	4	L	9	Outdoor Run #9
Outdoor Run #5	5		10	Outdoor Run #10

H S   Door   F

Door   L   Door   ↑
                             N

Cage   Food

Door

The numbered squares adjacent to each outdoor run mark the indoor runs. The storeroom is the area having four doors, wherein "H" represents a hot-water heater, "S" means sink and "F" symbolizes a furnace. "L" stands for overhead lighting fixtures throughout the building. Shelving could be installed on any of the storeroom walls except in the area occupied by the furnace. Office and/or grooming space can be added merely by increasing the size of the storeroom. Notice that enough aisle space exists between interior runs to allow you to open run doors opposite one another and still have enough room to walk past them. The following diagram illustrates how easily this layout could be expanded; note that the size of the storeroom would likely have to be expanded due to the increased number of runs.

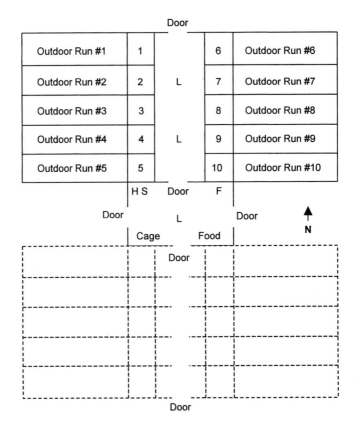

Mapping Out Your Ideas

I can barely draw a straight line, but I am fortunate to know more than one person who can create accurate images on paper. Such folks were a godsend when I was planning my kennel, and hopefully you are either talented and willing, or you know someone who is. It's one thing to mentally conceive several ideas around a central theme, but it's another to visualize the composite result with sufficient accuracy to allow you to confidently proceed to the construction phase.

First, draw your plans as best you can, specifying all dimensions, including such things as elevation and sloping. Then, unless you yourself are good at graphic design and representation, engage someone who can work from your sketches and make your ideas come to life on paper.

Location

Once you've decided how many runs your kennel will have and have created at least a rough sketch of the facility, it's time to determine location if you haven't already. This could be the first step, and in a sense it will be, as you likely already have a general notion about where you will build. But until you have determined the number of runs, which contributes to settling the kennel's overall size, selecting an exact site is difficult.

A primary consideration is the presence of trees. They not only can lend a restful, aesthetically pleasing quality to your operation, but can provide shade, security and windbreaks and can act as a sound deadener. If you have more than one possible site on which to erect your facility, it's probably best that you use the area near the most trees. Locate the kennel to take advantage of the trees' blessings in the pecking order given above: shade, security, windbreak, and sound suppression.

Construction and Materials
Walls

For my money, the optimal material for constructing exterior kennel walls is 8-inch-thick concrete block, reinforced with $1/2$-inch steel rebar and filled with concrete. For interior, non-load-bearing walls, I prefer 6-inch-thick blocks. Concrete blocks are fireproof, readily available and adaptable; they can be packed with granular insulation and, with proper reinforcement, are virtually dog-proof in terms of indestructibility. True, concrete-block porosity can make for a germ haven, but properly applied coatings of block-filler (which produces a semismooth surface) followed by multiple coats of industrial-grade enamel or acrylic paint, can greatly obviate that risk.

Another benefit to concrete-block buildings, especially those that are sealed with paint, is that they contain sound well. That can be a minus when you are in the building and several boarders decide to harmonize (which is why I keep a pair of shooter's ear protectors handy), but it's a plus from a neighbor's point of view and, long-term, that's a plus for you.

A drawback to concrete-block construction is that you will probably have to hire a professional to do the work. It isn't just the weight of the blocks that necessitates help, it's the fact that each block has to be positioned just so or you can wind up with a leaning tower of kennel. Blocks can be incorrectly placed in any of 16 ways (I'm told), and a recurring fraction-of-an-inch error starting at the foundation can expand to a glitch of several inches by the roof line.

A material to avoid in wall construction is wood. Not only is it vulnerable to fire, but even the hardest wood is not impervious to canine chewing or clawing. Wood is okay for ceiling and roof construction, provided the ceiling is painted with several coats of heavy enamel or acrylic paint to retard moisture and germs. Because wood is far more forgiving of slight errors than concrete block, you may be able to do some of the ceiling work yourself, thereby saving on construction costs.

Some kennel operators are sold on the idea of metal siding or roofing. My objections to it are that it is costly, dents easily, does not contain sound well, and is less than pleasing to the eye. Those drawbacks, and the fact that some kinds provide poor insulation against heat and cold, keep me from recommending the material.

Windows

Mount windows high enough that no dog can reach them. They should be openable, to permit periodic airing out, and lockable, for temperature control and security purposes. Slope the interior and exterior concrete footings at the base of each window to promote water runoff.

I know kennel owners who prefer not to have windows in their building, for a variety of reasons, usually cost. My thought is that the difference in expense between a few windows and the concrete blocks they replace is so slight as to be negligible, and the light and airy atmosphere windows provide is calming both for the dogs and for their owners.

Well-designed, well-placed kennel windows.

A Dutch door leading from the storeroom to the indoor kennel area.

Exterior Doors

Insulated metal doors (for human access) are my choice. They are durable, affordable and sanitary and do a good job of keeping the elements at bay, especially if you install a magnetic strip around the frame, which makes the door seal more tightly than nonmetal doors. My sole objection to insulated metal doors concerns the "metal" part: They can be dented.

Interior Doors

My preference for interior doors, which separate the indoor-run area from a storeroom or office, are wooden Dutch doors sealed with multiple coats of industrial-grade enamel or acrylic paint. Opening the top half of the door during the day promotes better air flow and facilitates allowing a selected dog to spend some time with you in the storeroom or office while enabling you to keep an eye and ear on the other boarders. Be sure to shut both halves of the door when you aren't around, lest a hairy Houdini escape from her run and hop into the storeroom to pig out on foodstuffs.

Whatever type of doors you select for exterior or interior purposes, make them at least 3 feet wide. Narrower widths are available at less cost, true, but have you ever tried to walk side by side with a Saint Bernard through a typical doorway? It can be quite an experience. The extra inches are also handy when toting 50-pound bags of food into the kennel.

Indoor/Outdoor Run-Access Doors

At a rate of one door per run, this equipment can quickly add up to a significant investment. Security and ease of use must remain foremost considerations, however, so don't skimp on these items.

The market offers a varied selection of styles and prices, but one of my preferences is for galvanized metal, vertically sliding doors, often termed "guillotine" doors. Though I abhor the label, I like the product for manageability, durability, security and cost. Each door is held in place by a long metal wall-mounted track on each side of each door. Attaching strong yet lightweight chain to the indoor top of each door and feeding it through a pulley above each indoor unit, ending within your reach near the entry door, provides an easy means of opening and closing each door without having to enter a run. Further, the doors can easily be locked open by clipping the chain to a spring-loaded lock attached to the top of each corresponding run. This allows boarders to spend time inside or outside according to their preference.

A drawback to guillotine doors is that a determined, powerful dog can literally tear them out of their tracks. I have encountered many canines with the ability but few with the inclination, however, and have housed those rare claustrophobic and/or destructive animals in high-security cages at night, each day allowing them time in runs with the access doors locked open.

Another type of guillotine door is made of lightweight yet super-durable, clear, space-age-type plastic. These doors are mounted as described above and offer as much insulating value as their metal cousins while also allowing sunlight into the kennel. Of course, they can also cause a bumped head now and then, until the dog realizes that not every-thing is as it seems—i.e., a door that appears open is actually closed—and they allow occupants to see out, which can make for a noisy kennel when a nearby rabbit decides to see how many dogs she can make sing.

Regarding the size of the doors, there are two considerations. First consider the size of the doorways (the actual openings in the wall). Mine are 28 inches high by 14 inches wide. I've found that these dimensions are adequate for even the largest dogs to gain entry, yet are small enough

Operated by overhead chain-pulley system, guillotine-type are my choice for run-access doors.

The capability to lock a run-access door open is a convenience for both the dog and you.

not to waste heating or air conditioning efforts. The dimensions of my guillotine doors themselves are 30 inches high by 16 inches wide.

At the exterior bottom of each doorway I installed a solid, concrete-block threshold 4 inches high to keep water and snow from the indoor run. This threshold block was slightly tilted toward the outside run to promote water runoff and drying.

Roofing

Rolled roofing is far less costly than shingles and is also easier to apply, which may allow you to install it yourself. Shingles are more vulnerable to damage, especially from wind, but on the other hand, they are easier to replace than are sections of rolled roofing. Properly applied, either presents a pleasing appearance.

A case can also be made for metal roofing. Its durability is unquestionable. My objections to it are that it isn't the best insulator in the world, its aesthetics are less than pleasing, and it tends to amplify sound rather than contain it.

Ceiling

A plywood ceiling is acceptable in a boarding kennel. The material is inexpensive, durable, and reasonably easy to shape and handle. Paint the ceiling with multiple coats of high-gloss white enamel to provide an easily cleanable surface that reflects light well.

Flooring

Concrete is the way to go. It's readily available, durable, easily cleaned and affordable. Its drawbacks are that it is only moderately effective in shutting out heat and cold, and—like concrete block—you may have to hire skilled labor to pour and finish it. Make sure that reinforcing steel mesh is laid in the formed areas prior to pouring the pads to reduce the likelihood of major cracking and separating.

You may decide to paint your interior flooring. I did and it was a mistake. Concrete takes paint well enough, but paint does not withstand constant wearing from canine nails. Bare concrete is not very attractive, but it is more so than bare concrete from which paint has been randomly scratched away.

In place of paint, you might want to consider hardened polymer coatings that apply much like paint. They eliminate the need for any additional preservatives, paints or chew-stop preparations, they adhere well to wood or concrete, and they are impact resistant. They have high thermal reflective insulator properties, provide a moisture-barrier, and have effective germicidal and fungicidal qualities. If you opt for this type of flooring application, which is available in several colors, including clear, be sure to select the antiskid style to provide safer footing.

Heating and Cooling

The need for each is directly related to your climate. At my kennel in northern Wyoming at one-mile elevation, fans sufficed in place of air conditioning since large trees gave my kennels good shade from the afternoon sun, which was seldom very hot to start with. In other regions of the country, however, lack of air conditioning could be life-threatening.

The need for heat during Wyoming winters was quite another matter as subzero temperatures were common and prolonged. You probably already know whether you prefer propane, natural gas, electricity or another source (like solar panels) to heat your kennels and power your water heater; the availability of energy types and costs varies regionally. I opted for a propane furnace and located it in the storeroom where it forced heated air through an overhead duct into the kennels. Small ceiling fans gently blew the air downward where it was circulated through a grill in the storeroom door to the furnace's air intake. My water heater, a 40-gallon model that seemed adequate for my 10-run facility, also was powered by propane. During harsh weather I housed as many dogs as possible in the kennel's south-facing runs, restricted the north side to thick-coated animals, and kept everyone indoors as much as possible.

Rather than provide you with a semi-learned discussion of BTUs (British Thermal Units) versus square or cubic feet, I suggest you do what I did: Contact an energy professional.

In-Floor Radiant Heating

Advances in materials and engineering made this affordable for the small-kennel owner. How valuable is this? Not very if you live in the south, but in the northern climates it's a treasure, especially to dogs suffering from arthritis or hip dysplasia. Yes, this increases construction expense and the ongoing costs of heating the water, but the result can be a much warmer dog.

Installation seems simple in concept, but calls for skilled labor. Essentially, warm water from a dedicated (i.e., separate) heater is circulated through specialized tubing laid under the interior runs. The tubing should be laid atop stabilized wire mesh and fastened to it before the concrete is poured, to reduce the possibility of damage to the tubing during the pour. The loops of tubing should be zigzagged about 10 inches apart under each run and should lie 3 inches below the concrete surface, though this can vary according to the type of tubing material and the severity of climate. If the concept has appeal, contact a plumber who is experienced with this type of installation.

Refrigeration

Whether you need a kennel refrigerator depends on your climate, size of the operation and personal preference. As I fed most of my boarders dry food (kibble), the need for refrigeration was rare, occasioned by old dogs who couldn't chew well. When I needed to refrigerate leftovers, I used my house's unit. This led a few folks to chuckle until I pointed out that this was what I would do for my own dogs if I didn't own a kennel. I lost a few potential dinner guests that way, but I've never cared much for overly persnickety folks anyway.

Interior Lighting

All interior lighting should be mounted on the ceiling. A boarding kennel is not a place for table, pole or hanging lamps—the risk of breakage is high and accidents could injure boarders. Two hallway-centered overhead fixtures, each containing a 200-watt bulb, adequately illuminate a 15- by 20-foot room. In choosing the style of fixture, since the amount of light emitted is more important than decor, I prefer the clear, rounded-end variety that resembles a glass jar. Yes, glass is breakable, but few plastic fixtures can handle the heat generated by 200-watt bulbs.

One style of lighting to avoid is fluorescent. The stuff is hard on the eyes, and dangers from fumes and glass alike can result if a tube breaks—fluorescent tubes tend to explode, rather than merely shatter, when broken.

Exterior Lighting

Exterior lighting is a convenience, but its primary function is security. While it's convenient to be able to see what you are doing (and where you are stepping) when cleaning runs after dark, it's more important to be able to illuminate the kennel and adjacent grounds with the flick of a switch. Wiring should be installed so that the exterior lights can be controlled from the kennel itself and from your house. Again, that's a convenience, but security is still the main purpose.

Overhead interior lighting.
Note the overhead fan suspended
between the light fixtures.

A close-up of the overhead fan suspended between the light fixtures.
Surprisingly, this small unit provides adequate air circulation for this kennel's
interior, which measures approximately 20 feet by 15 feet by 8 feet.

Exterior lighting for the kennels and the training yard.

Interior run height should not be greater than 4 feet.

Inside Run Dividers

Use 6-inch-thick concrete block to separate indoor, side-by-side runs. This results in each interior run having solid walls on three sides, which not only prevents cleaning solutions and such from flowing into adjacent runs, but also provides occupants with a measure of emotional security. They don't feel so exposed, as they would were the indoor runs separated by chainlink or similar material. While no dog can see another dog next to him, which makes for a quieter kennel, boarders can see other animals on the other side of the aisle through the indoor-run gates, which lessens feelings of isolation.

Like the building's exterior and interior walls, the run dividers should be reinforced with $1/2$-inch rebar and filled with concrete for maximum strength. Eight-inch-thick concrete blocks could be used as interior-run separators, though doing so would constitute a waste of space and materials. Don't use blocks narrower than 6 inches, however. I doubt that any dog could destroy a properly reinforced wall of 2-inch-thick blocks, for instance, but a large, powerful canine could significantly damage and perhaps weaken the structure.

Interior runs need be no higher than 4 feet. Keeping the interior-run height low not only makes for much better air flow throughout the kennel building, but makes for a quieter kennel as well, since the boarders are more constrained in their activities. They can get all the jump-around exercise they need when they are outside.

Outside Run Dividers

Though it is easily installed, chainlink should not be the sole means of separating runs: Liquids can flow from one run to another, and the incidence of fence fighting is much higher. Concrete block or poured concrete dividers eliminate the possibility of liquids flowing to a neighboring run, and they also greatly discourage fence fighting.

My outside runs were separated from one another by placing 4-foot-high chainlink panels atop 2-foot-high dividers fashioned from 4-inch-thick concrete block, which were then filled with concrete. The result, of course, is a total run height of 6 feet.

The chainlink panels should not merely rest atop the concrete-block (or poured concrete) dividers; they should be attached to them. If the panels are not attached to the dividers, a large, powerful dog could push a panel, especially near its center, far enough away from a divider to catch a paw between the panel and the divider as the panel springs back.

Outside run dividers.

Preventing chainlink panel's side-to-side movement by using metal plumber's tape to attach each panel to the concrete-block divider.

Attaching panels to dividers is easily done by looping several inches of plumber's metal strapping tape over a panel's bottom rail and pressing the ends of the tape into the divider while the concrete is still wet (see photograph). At my kennels I spaced the strapping tape every 4 feet.

The market offers metal panels that attach to the lower part of each chainlink panel, thereby separating boarders, but in times of high heat these panels can become quite hot and could burn a dog. Also, although metal panels can alleviate fence fighting, they are ineffective against preventing liquids from flowing from run to run.

Inside-Run Tops

My indoor runs are topped with lightweight mesh fencing nailed to wooden frames made from 2-inch by 2-inch lumber; the frames match the dimensions of each run top. The frames are held in place by window locks attached to 2-inch by 2-inch strips that separate each run top from the one next to it.

Incidentally, though covered inside-run tops may seem a handy location to store large objects (airline cages, for example), I recommend against placing such items there. Doing so would block light from illuminating the run, and things above a dog tend to make her nervous. Further, it is unwise to place small, lightweight items (such as leashes or blankets) on the run tops as the run's occupant may attempt to pull the objects into her run. A dog may not be able to do so, of course—the run-top fencing should see to that—but in trying the animal could injure herself or damage the item or the run top.

Outside-Run Overhead Fencing

Why, you may wonder, is it necessary to put fencing across the tops of runs that are 6 feet high? True, a dog would probably have a heck of a time jumping over such a height, but don't presume that cats are the only housepets who can climb. I have seen more than one dog scramble up a chainlink run panel.

Also, the overhead fencing serves a second security purpose: It lessens the chance that some deranged soul would be successful in hurling a tainted substance (like poisoned meat) into a run.

The fencing across my outside runs is lightweight wire mesh that I attached to the vertical run panels using electric-fence wire, which is strong enough wire for the job yet is thin and malleable enough to make working with it easy. It occurred to me to use chainlink tops, but they are expensive and are difficult to handle, owing to their weight. Using

Note that there is no need to tightly attach the overhead fencing to the chainlink side panel.

lightweight wire-mesh fencing may seem inadequate until one realizes that no dog is capable of climbing a chainlink side panel and hanging there for the time it would take for her to chew through the overhead material.

Run Gates

Run gates, interior and exterior, should be fabricated from chainlink. Their bottom support rails should be raised $2^1/2$ inches from the concrete to allow sufficient room for hosing solids from the runs into a clean-out trough without allowing room for a large dog to catch a paw under a rail or for a small animal to escape. Outdoor gates should be 6 feet high so you don't have to stoop when entering or departing a run. Indoor gates should be 4 feet high, like the indoor runs, but mounted in 6-foot-high frames, with the excess or 2-foot open part of each frame being above each gate. If 6-foot-high gates were used, access to the area above the run would be blocked by chainlink. If you use 4-foot-high gates mounted in 4-foot high frames, you would be forced to bend over to enter a run.

Two locks are needed for each gate. Use the padlock when you're going to be off-property for a time. The other lock, which is merely a curved piece of metal inserted in the lock aperture such that a dog cannot dislodge it, is for any other time.

Chainlink Mesh Sizes

Chainlink mesh sizes vary greatly. Too large a mesh can allow a small dog to lodge her head in a square, while too small a gap can enable a large dog to wedge a paw. Though the "right" size depends upon whom you talk to, my mesh preference is 2 inches square.

Run Surfaces

Of the three most common types of run surfaces—dirt, gravel, and concrete—my preference in boarding-kennel construction is concrete, for two reasons: security and ease of cleaning and disinfecting. Security is provided by concrete, as I have yet to meet a dog that could dig through it. I have encountered many for whom a dirt or gravel surface presented a challenge if not an outright invitation. Ease in cleaning and disinfecting because, well—can you imagine trying to scrub a graveled or dirt-surfaced run?

A disadvantage to concrete is that it's hard on the legs, joints and feet of dogs confined on it for extended periods. This problem can be circumvented to a degree by placing resting pads in the indoor runs and by allowing time in an exercise yard. Another drawback is that the material is more costly than gravel or dirt, especially given the fact that skilled labor is needed to form the pads, pour them and finish the surface.

Run surfaces—both interior and exterior—should be sloped away from the kennel walls at the rate of $1/4$ inch per foot of length. This allows urine and cleaning substances to flow away from the building, but the pitch is not so great as to make for difficult footing, even when runs are wet or icy. The width dimension of the runs should be dead level to prevent liquids from flowing into adjacent runs. The soil beneath the concrete should be compacted for stability, and the depth of the concrete should be between 4 and 6 inches, depending on pad size and on the severity of winters and the stability of the ground in your area. If you are uncertain, thicker is generally better, but don't go to extremes. Be safe by checking with a local concrete driveway contractor.

Exterior run surfaces should be configured and poured as a pad, not as a separate pour for each run. Pad pours are generally easier and are usually less expensive.

Once you have determined the length and width of your outdoor run pads, add 12 inches each to the overall length and the overall width. For instance, a pad for five runs, each of which is 4 feet wide by 16 feet long, should measure 21 feet wide (4-feet-per-run wide times 5 runs, plus 12 inches) by 17 feet long (16 feet long plus 12 inches).* The purpose is to provide a 6-inch safety margin from side to side, and a foot of room for a clean-out trough at the end of the runs.

Waste Disposal

Though local public-health dictates may make the decision for you, a common boarding-kennel solution to the need for efficient waste disposal is an underground septic system. A clean-out trough, at the end of and perpendicular to each series of runs, slopes toward a drain at a rate of $1/4$ inch for each foot of length. The drain empties into a septic tank that drains into a leach field. The septic tank should be periodically pumped out to lessen the strain on it and on the leach system.

Computing tank size can be tricky. They are generally sized by the number of bedrooms and bathrooms in a home. A three-bedroom, two-bathroom house usually gets a 1,200-gallon tank because it is assumed that four people will be using the house. Figure your waste material according to the number of dogs you will board at capacity and how

---

*Please note that I am speaking here in round numbers for simplicity: Runs measuring 4 feet wide separated by 4-inch-wide concrete block dividers will actually measure 3 feet, 10 inches wide.

An outdoor clean-out trough abutting the run pad.

A hazard: leaves collecting in the drain. Flushed into the system in quantity, leaves can plug a leach field.

After the first concrete pour, which is for the kennel's interior flooring, things begin to make a little more sense.

As the walls begin to rise you may get flashes of how the finished building will appear.

Pretty soon the building has a roof.

Then it is time to begin work on laying out the outdoor run dividers, which were concrete blocks that we angle-cut so that the finished dividers would stand level, not sloped like the concrete pads.

Once the dividers are erected . . .

. . . it's time to install the chainlink panels.

Then a little more paint, a perimeter fence surrounding a red-shale walkway, and before you know it you're visiting with your first boarder!

Designing and Building a Boarding Kennel 71

With proper plumbing, septic gases should not be able to enter the kennel building. Using an interior-drain cap, like the one shown, ensures they can't.

much waste you will have to dispose of. Most counties require a health department permit for a septic tank.

To be sure, this is an expensive system, but it can pay for itself over time in saved trash-hauling fees. It also makes for much easier run cleaning. The traditional alternative is surrounding each run pad with a bed of drainage gravel several inches deep and hosing urine and cleaning solutions into it and scooping or shoveling feces into several large trash cans that have been double-lined with heavy-duty bags. The first time a bag ruptures while being moved, however, resulting in its contents being strewn about, not only can lead one to think dark thoughts, but moreover can induce no less than a longing for the convenience of a septic system.

Perimeter Fencing

To say that there are more kinds and styles of fences than there are breeds of dogs may overstate the case, but not by much. For surrounding a kennel, however, there are only three good options: chainlink, wire mesh or wood.

Chainlink is durable and adapts well to boarding kennel usage. It is also expensive and—unless preformed panels are used—is not the easiest type of fencing to install.

Wire mesh fencing, especially the *non-climb* variety, is also durable. It thwarts canine visions of escape as well as chainlink does, but it is more affordable and easier for most people to install. Though a droopy non-climb fence would suggest sloppy workmanship, don't stretch perimeter fencing until it is razor tight: Non-climb fencing with a little give is harder for a dog to climb than that attached as tight as a drumhead.

Avoid lightweight-gauge, woven-wire fencing. Most dogs cannot chew through it, but repeated jumping against it can cause the wires to separate. It is also vulnerable to rusting.

Though any type of wire fencing—chainlink or wire mesh—does nothing to dampen sound, wooden fence material does. Unfortunately, wooden fences can be vulnerable to chewing, climbing, wind and fire. They also require periodic maintenance in the form of painting or staining and reattaching loose boards.

If the type of fence you choose to erect around your kennels necessitates the use of wooden posts, use materials that either have been treated against moisture and insects or are naturally impervious to such problems. The only aspect of fencing that is more difficult than original construction is that of having to replace rotted posts. Also, set at least the corner posts and the gateposts in concrete and brace them well (as described in the section on fencing and gate materials in Chapter 1, "Designing and Building a Home Kennel"), the idea being to promote stability and longevity.

Everything about this boarding kennel's appearance says "Home."

Regardless of the type of fence you choose, guard against tunneling by burying an 18-inch-wide strip of rust-resistant, wire-mesh fencing inside and along the fence line. Place the fencing flat and parallel to the fence at a depth of 4 inches.

Exercise Yards

Do you plan to have a few? Provided they are escape-proof, such areas can be worthwhile additions to any boarding kennel. They afford pooch a chance to get off the concrete for a while and to run and stretch her legs while freeing her mind. Of course, escorting dogs to and from the yards takes additional time and effort, but the benefits to the animals' physical, mental and emotional well-being, in terms of exercise, a break from the boredom of confinement and a measure of relative freedom, are well worth it.

Two problems attend the exercise yard concept. First, soil can't be as effectively disinfected as concrete. That is why a dog should be given run of a yard only after she has eliminated. She may still mark areas of the yard, but that's dogs for you. Second, risk of injury or escape is greater. This is why I won't allow yard time to diggers or fence climbers, suspected or confirmed. You may also wish not to grant yard time to dogs who won't come when called, necessitating that you chase them.

Landscaping and Decor

Boarded dogs could care less that your property's lawns are well maintained, that you have flower beds, or that the kennel building and the outside-run dividers are painted in an inviting, coordinated color scheme. The ideas behind creating an appearance as appealing to the eye as the kennel's comfort is to dogs is to put people at ease, specifically owners. Because a nicely decorated kennel gives them a sense of comfort and confidence about the care their pets receive, the owners—perhaps without conscious intent or realization—transmit these feelings to their dogs, who are generally receptive to such messages. This makes it easier for a dog to accept being away from her family, which is a primary goal.

Another reason behind landscaping and decor is to provide you with a work environment in which you can take pride. To some folks a career that frequently includes cleaning up dog droppings would be seen as something of a sentence. You and I don't look at it that way, of course, and a facility whose appointments suggest a positive, feel-good-about-the-place attitude can help make sure we never do.

Set gate and corner posts in concrete for stability and permanence.

A handy type of latch for yard gates. The latch snaps shut automatically from the weight of the gate pushing against it. The latch can also be secured with a padlock.

Decorations such as a birdbath and a flowerpot can lend a homey touch to your kennels.

In selecting colors for your kennel, avoid dark hues. They can lend a foreboding atmosphere to your building, and they don't reflect light well. However, don't go to the other extreme by selecting hospital white. We want to communicate sanitary conditions, yes, but not cold sterility.

Sign

Like your choice of kennel name, the appearance of your kennel's sign can help you or hurt you. As it's likely the first expression of your business that a client will see, it's that person's first contact with your operation and contributes to the customer's first impression of your facility.

Your sign should be professional in appearance. That's not to say that it has to be done by a professional. If you can do a good job of it, there's no need to hire someone to make a sign for you. At the same time, if shaping and painting are not among your talents, you'd be money ahead to contract a professional's services instead of winding up with a sign that looks like I did it.

Avoid a specific breed shape or breed artwork for your sign, for the same reasons that it is unwise to include a specific breed as part of your kennel name. It is never shrewd to exclude by omission any segment of your potential clientele.

Should you have a sign at all? Usually a sign identifying your business is worthwhile, but in some instances one can actually be more of a problem than a solution. My driveway, for example, begins at a considerable distance from my home and kennel. Placing a sign at the beginning of my driveway could easily lead to the sign hanging in some college student's dorm room. A second reason why I don't have a sign is that I don't want puppies to be dumped under the cattle guard separating my driveway from the county road. Some people do things like that.

Labor

In this chapter I've alluded more than once to the notion that in some phases of construction you may be able to perform the work yourself to reduce expense. Underscore the "may" in that observation, however. Do-it-yourselfing is merely an option, not a recommendation. I know from personal experience that a person with decidedly limited construction skills can surprise him- or herself with what comes from a little research, some hard yet satisfying work, and occasional coaching from construction professionals. I also know that designing and erecting a kennel is quite different from building, say, a garage. Sloped concrete pads and raised grooming tubs are but two extraordinary elements that make kennel construction unique. The trick is to undertake only those jobs that you understand and can physically handle safely. There are many risks in construction work, from power tools, ladders and materials, to enumerate but a few sources of potential disaster. There is also the danger that you might wind up spending more on error correction than you would have spent hiring professionals in the first place. Whether to involve yourself is largely a common sense decision, and should be made in tandem with the notion that if you have the slightest doubt, stay with what you are good at, like dealing with our best friend, and leave construction to those who know how.

In hiring people to construct your kennels, it may be that you already know several professionals and know that they deliver on their promises: solid results at an agreed price by the date specified. If you are shopping for help, however, investigate thoroughly all comers before committing yourself. Request a list of folks they have worked for, and ask those people for their evaluations. A most revealing query can be, "Would you hire this person to do the same job again?" Also, visit with building material suppliers and ask for their impressions of the individual's work. Listen for what the suppliers do not say, be aware when issues are sidestepped, and if you often hear a variation on "Oh, he's okay, I guess," keep looking.

I'm neither a mason, plumber, electrician nor finished-work carpenter, but I was able to smooth out the trench for pouring the footers and clean up the mortar spatters.

I installed spatters, installed the ceiling insulation, and painted the building. Lots of backaches, but lots of satisfaction, too.

Get it in writing. Handshake contracts have their place, but you should obtain written bids outlining the work to be done, the materials to be used, the total costs to you, when payments are due and the promised date of completion. Also, secure a waiver from anyone you hire, absolving you of any and all liability pertaining to on-the-job injuries from the beginning of the world until the date of the work's completion. Be sure that any contractor you engage carries his own health, accident and liability insurance. Don't just ask if he carries insurance: Get the insurers' names and verify the facts with them.

Housing for Destructive Dogs

Some dogs are incredibly destructive. I'm not referring to water-bucket spillers or blanket nibblers. They're easy to deal with: Refill the bucket and remove the blanket. The destroyers I have in mind can rip run-access doors from their tracks and make valiant attempts at chainlink destruction. While such animals are thankfully few and far between (and whether you're willing to accept such boarders is a decision only you can make), housing them calls for extraordinary measures. You must not only preserve and protect your kennels, but also must protect the dog from himself.

A male German Shepherd created this damage to a run gate in less than 10 minutes.

Three views of "The Cage" and its latching and locking systems.

Though an airline cage may successfully contain a destructive dog, I have seen large, powerful animals of this persuasion pop a cage door within minutes. Stainless-steel wire cages are equally ineffective. So what does one do?

I contracted a local welding company to build an escape-proof cage. Measuring 3 feet high by 2 feet wide by 4 feet deep, it was constructed of $1/2$-inch iron rebar spaced at 2-inch intervals. My reaction upon seeing the finished product was that the dog who could escape from this cage would scare me half to death. A galvanized metal pan, removable to facilitate cleaning, lines the bottom of the enclosure to provide as much comfort as possible. Owing to its weight, the cage cannot be tipped over.

Regardless of how you plan to deal with destructive dogs, any boarding kennel should have at least one escape-proof, indestructible enclosure.

Feline Facilities?

Here is an end-of-chapter thought in the form of a question: Do you intend to board cats as well as dogs? If so, be sure to allow additional room for installation of however many banks of cat cages you intend to have. These cages should be in a room separate from where you house dogs, and should be large enough that the cats can move about and be active. Cats may appear to need less exercise than dogs, but the reality is that they are just more patient when faced with utter boredom.

You will also need additional food and water bowls (as described in Chapter 5, "Equipment and Supplies"), litter boxes and additional room for food and litter storage.

*R*eflection

The method of the enterprising is to plan with audacity, and execute with vigor; to sketch out a map of possibilities, and then to treat them as probabilities.

CHRISTIAN NELSON BOVEE

Setting Up Your Business

Choosing a Kennel Name: A Word on Marketing

How important is the name you give your business? If you offer top-flight facilities and service at reasonable prices, does the name matter all that much? Consider: before RCA signed Elvis Presley to a recording contract, another major record company turned him down. One of its executives said that no one with a name like *that* would ever make it in show business. Granted, it wasn't the smartest thing the company ever did—the decision probably led to a good deal of finger pointing in its boardrooms over the years—but you get the idea: a name that sounds wrong can blind people to a business's attributes.

When naming your kennel, keep four concepts in mind:

- Mass appeal
- Clarity
- Memorability
- Singleness of purpose

A name like "Grannie Grump's Pooch Parlor and Storm-Door Company" violates all four. Grannie may be the salt of the earth, as friendly, conscientious and caring a person as you'd ever meet, but the images her name conjures up suggest otherwise. Just as it lacks mass appeal, "Pooch Parlor" doesn't represent clarity in wording. The phrase could signify a boarding kennel, but it could just as easily refer to a grooming salon. The name is too long to be memorable, and its disparate concepts violate singleness of purpose.

Mass appeal means choosing a name that makes most people feel comfortable. Your name and the word "kennels" might do the trick, especially if you are regionally known as a dog person. Or you might incorporate area themes into the name. Avoid overused geographic references, however. Several businesses in my locale use the *Cloud Peak* appellation, so it isn't one I would consider for my kennel. Also, don't use a name whose meaning can change over time. *Edge-O'-Town Kennels* sounds fine today, but what if years later community growth moves the edge of town away from your location?

Preserve *clarity* by communicating the nature of your business through its name. "McGee's" might work in some instances, like a bar, a restaurant or a hair-styling salon, but a name like "McGee's Boarding Kennels" removes all doubt. "McGee's Pet Haven" might sound okay, but "Pet Haven" could suggest a pet cemetery, a ghastly link for a boarding kennel.

Make the name *memorable*, easy for your clients to call to mind. A short and simple name is usually preferable to a long or complex one.

Singleness of purpose gives you an edge over vets who board. Because boarding isn't a sideline with you, say so in your kennel name. "McGee's Boarding Kennels" and "McGee's Dog Boarding" both express singleness of

Grandma's kitchen?
Or a groomer's bathing area?
Do it right and some folks
may have trouble differentiating
between the two.

purpose. Incidentally, a name like "McGee's Dog Boarding and Grooming" doesn't violate the singleness of purpose concept since many dog owners view the two activities as so closely related as to be inseparable.

If yours is a breeding and boarding kennel, avoid linking the fact that you raise puppies with the name of your boarding operation, lest clients think your priorities are divided. Some might worry that their pets' needs would play second fiddle to your pups'. Also, consider another way in which linking your boarding-kennel name with a breed can have a negative effect. Let's say you breed German Shepherds. That's fine, but to name your facility "McGee's German Shepherds and Boarding Kennel" is to risk losing the small-dog crowd, as well as owners who are intimidated by large dogs generally or German Shepherds specifically. Likewise, many large-dog owners seeing an ad for "McGee's Toy Poodles and Boarding Kennels" may keep looking. You and I know that a dog is a dog is a dog, but some owners would deem such a notion fallacious, if not blasphemous. Unless you intend to house only certain breeds or sizes of dogs, take care not to limit your clientele unintentionally.

Finally, when naming your kennel, don't contract a case of the cutes. A friend was going to name her facility "The Flea Circus." Sure, it's a "cute" idea—you and I might get a chuckle out of it—but I wonder how many potential clients would be similarly amused.

Deciding How Much to Charge
Basic Price Structure

How much will you charge? How will you base your rates? According to sizes or breeds? If you're new to the business, the first question has already been answered for you: Newcomers are ill-advised to charge more than established area rates. Your facilities may be the nicest around, but you're still the new kid on the block. To attract business you may have to appeal to an owner's pocketbook first. Your runs may be worth more than those of your competitors, but not to people who have never seen them. And if you start out charging more than established operations, few folks will see them. If many locals are satisfied with your competitors, you have to offer something to get them to try your kennels. Low rates are a quick way to get the ball rolling. You can always raise your fees once you have established yourself and have a solid, loyal following.

If you opt for a rate structure based on the size of the dog, keep it simple. Don't make it strict or confusing. A rate structure divided into too many categories can make some owners suspect you are trying to get to them. I charge one rate for any dog up to the approximate size of a

Cocker Spaniel, and another rate for any dog larger than that. A friend charges the same for any dog, reasoning that all dogs require the same amount of work and take up the same amount of space. He's right and wrong at the same time because it's a matter of perception. A Miniature Pinscher owner might feel overcharged at paying the same rate as the owner of a St. Bernard, and it's the owner's perception that makes him or her decide whether to board with you.

Discounts

A client booking space for an extended period may request a discount. First, what is an "extended period"? Some owners feel it's anything beyond a week, but I don't see it that way. To my view it's a month or longer, and yes, I will reduce the daily rate for such a reservation. However, I advise the client that the discount applies only if the dog is with me for the total time reserved. If an owner reserves a run for six weeks but returns after only three, the rate reverts to normal and I adjust the account accordingly. I also tell the owner my terms for discounted rates: Half of the total amount is due when pooch arrives, and the balance is payable when he leaves. This way I don't have so many dollars on the line if the person returns early and tries to push for the discount anyway.

Now, you have to use some common sense here. If a client books a run for eight weeks, and on that basis you grant a discounted rate, are you going to cancel the agreement if he returns five days early? I wouldn't. Sure, I could, but I've already made good money from the client, and inflexibility could cost me his future business and that of his friends as well.

Some owners want a break because they bring the dog's food from home. As I tell these owners, though, it's actually more work for me to have to keep track of who is being fed what than to feed all boarders the same food. The different foods also take up more space in my storeroom. For these reasons I don't grant discounts to owners who bring their own vittles. To my knowledge I've never lost a client over this policy.

A final discount-related question is: "Do you give your friends a break?" I do. "Even during your busier periods?" Yes. Though I can make a case for keeping business matters business, it's a personal choice with which I am comfortable.

Fees for Additional Services

In addition to the basic fee structure you establish for basic boarding services, you should decide what other special services you are willing to provide upon request, such as administering medication or doing lightweight grooming, whether or not you will charge for them, and how much you'll charge.

If a dog becomes ill and you have to take him to a vet, don't charge the client for the transporting service. Sure, it says in the boarding contract that you can, but my experience is that such events happen so rarely that it's better to settle for having the client's goodwill. If an owner asks, "What do I owe you for driving pooch to the vet?" an answer of, "Forget it. I'm glad I could help," will do far more for your business long-term than a few short-term dollars ever could.

Some boarding-kennel operators charge for giving medications. "It takes extra time, you know." Sure it does. At least 20 seconds. Anyone who can't give a pill, a liquid, or ear or eye drops in that amount of time hasn't been in the business long and won't be without adjusting their nickel-and-dime attitude. Give pooch his pill or whatever and be grateful for his company.

You may decide that you want to offer basic grooming services for boarders. You probably can safely do so without alienating the goodwill of local groomers who might otherwise see you as competition which, of course, could lead them not to send referrals your way. Coat clipping is out of the question, of course, but few groomers will be upset because you do bathing, brushing or nail trimming. Those are services that many people expect a boarding kennel to offer. Be sure to obtain the owner's written approval and release of liability for any sort of grooming, however. I know of one case where a dog's nail was clipped too short and the nail started to bleed after the owner took the animal home later that day. The kennel operator was successfully sued for the services of a veterinarian and for the cost of professionally cleaning the owner's carpet.

Marketing Your Business
Running Advertisements

Kennel operators often must select an advertising medium—radio, television, print or Internet—based on cost: Few small boarding kennels can afford TV ads. Determining the most productive type of advertisement, splashy and ornate versus modest and unadorned, is often a function of locale: Certain advertising formats are more apropos in some regions than in others. But remember one key to effective advertising: constantly keeping your business's name in front of the public. True, it's wise to run test ads in various media occasionally, if for no other reason than to determine effectiveness. But you should have a core advertising program, even if only in local classified sections, and you should run those ads year in and year out.

The Power of Word of Mouth

A second form of marketing is of the make-or-break variety: word of mouth. Prime-time TV advertising won't save a kennel that the public perceives as dirty, poorly run or generally uncaring about its boarders. Clients often tell me, "My dog likes coming out here. She gets excited when we get within about a mile of the place." People saying such things to me are communicating the same message to their friends, and that's not only a humbling compliment but the best kind of advertising around.

Printing Business Cards

Do you need to go to the expense of having business cards? I wouldn't try to run a boarding kennel without them. You may not need fold-over cards, resplendent in several colors with raised lettering and photographs, but a single or two-sided printed card stating at least your name and your kennel's name, phone number and address is a must. Give a few to clients as they pick up their pets, saying, "Please tell your friends," and offer cards to dog-related businesses, including veterinarians, in your locale. Don't make your cards available to slipshod businesses, though; that could taint you.

Participating in Community Events

You can greatly enhance your kennel's renown by participating in local dog-related activities, such as vaccination clinics, 4-H dog projects and AKC fun matches. Not only can such ventures be enjoyable for their own sakes, but participating in community dog programs also puts you more in the public eye and heightens your "dog person" status. It gets your name around.

Direct Mailing

Mailing material to prospective customers and existing customers is an easy way to promote your business. For my existing customers, for example, I send out two types of mailings: Christmas cards and tip sheets.

I send a Christmas card to every dog boarded with me during the preceding year. I address the envelope not to the owner but to the animal, as in "Buckwheat Jones." I started the practice partly out of sentiment—the holidays are for dogs, too, you know—and as a way of thanking the owners for their business. I didn't realize at the time what an impact it would have. As you know, many businesses send cards, calendars and such during the holiday season. The practice has become so routine that most of us can't remember which companies sent us what last December. But very few people will forget who sent their pet a holiday greeting, and as such it is a tremendous public relations concept.

With dogs that are old or in ill health, however, I make darn sure the animal is still on the planet before sending the card. We've all lost pets, and you can imagine how heartbreaking it would be for an owner of a deceased pupper to receive a cheery greeting addressed to the dog. Further, when I learn that a pet who has been boarded with me has passed away, I send the owner a sympathy card.

Periodically I mail clients information about *Canis familiaris*. I avoid complex or controversial topics, preferring instead to discuss such issues as the benefits of regular exercise, the dangers of feeding chocolate to our best friend or leaving him in a closed vehicle during hot weather, the importance of annual vaccinations and heartworm preventative, answers to often-asked questions about canine behavior, and so forth. These mailings are simply worded on a single folded page, with just enough artwork to be eye-catching. My kennel's name and return address are set in a distinctive typeface in the hope that the mailing won't be confused with junk mail and consigned to the circular file.

Reflection

Don't be afraid to take a big step if one is indicated. You can't cross a chasm in two small jumps.

DAVID LLOYD GEORGE

Equipment and Supplies

The general public might be amazed at the amount and types of equipment needed to run a boarding kennel. Of course, major items such as heating and air-conditioning units, a water heater, adjustable shelving, a telephone and a sink are necessary for most boarding kennel operations, but none of those are peculiar to the business. It's the list of distinctive-to-the-trade items that might surprise you, and you'll need to know about them in order to properly stock and equip your kennel.

Food- and Water-Related Supplies

Choosing the right supplies for providing food and water to your boarders are just as important as choosing the right construction materials. Here's a list of the basics you'll need to have:

❑ Stainless steel feeding bowls that are unbreakable and easy to clean. One of each size—one pint, one quart and two quart—per run should provide an adequate inventory. For identification, use a permanent marker to sequentially number each bowl according to the number of runs you have. Write the number on the external bottom of each bowl to prevent dogs from licking the ink as they might were you to number the sides.

It's difficult to have too much shelving in a kennel.

Food bowls and other supplies arranged on shelves on which run numbers have been painted.

- ❏ Galvanized or heavy-plastic garbage cans to store food and repel pests and moisture. Label each container and lid as to its contents. Label the cans as well—lids can get switched.
- ❏ Plastic, 2-cup-capacity food scoops for dry dogfood, one per food storage container
- ❏ Can opener for canned dogfood
- ❏ Spoons and forks for serving canned dogfood
- ❏ Stainless-steel water buckets: one per run, plus two extras. As you did for the food/water bowls, write the run number on the external bottom of each bucket.

Medical Supplies

Every boarding operation needs a first-aid kit containing at least the following items:

- ❏ A watch with a seconds indicator
- ❏ Adhesive tape ($1/2$-inch, 1-inch and 2-inch widths)
- ❏ Alcohol
- ❏ Adhesive bandages of various sizes
- ❏ Blankets
- ❏ Burn ointment
- ❏ Cloth towels
- ❏ Electric clippers
- ❏ Electric heating pad
- ❏ First-aid chart (see the Appendix)
- ❏ Sterilized gauze pads of various sizes
- ❏ Hemostats
- ❏ Hot water bottle
- ❏ Hydrogen peroxide
- ❏ Ice pack
- ❏ Lengths of rope
- ❏ Elastic bandages of various widths
- ❏ Matches
- ❏ Merthiolate
- ❏ Muzzles of various sizes
- ❏ High-intensity penlight
- ❏ Quik-Stop (a dry powder to halt minor bleeding, as from a broken nail or one clipped too closely)
- ❏ Sterilized rolled gauze

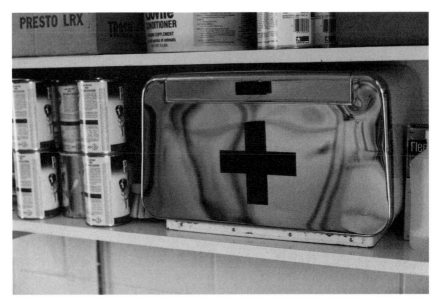

This breadbox makes an excellent container for first-aid supplies.

❏ Razor blades (single-edged)
❏ Scissors (three varieties: straight-bladed, angled and blunt-tipped)
❏ Splint material—ask your veterinarian for the proper kind
❏ Stabilizing transport board with security restraints and hand grips (like a stretcher, but solid; often made from plywood or high-impact plastic and covered with canvas or similar material)
❏ Sterilized syringes of various sizes
❏ Two dog thermometers
❏ Tourniquet material
❏ Tweezers
❏ Local veterinarian's phone numbers
❏ Two reference books and more than a passing familiarity with their contents:
    ❏ *Dog Owner's Home Veterinary Handbook* (by Carlson and Giffin)
    ❏ *Medical & Genetic Aspects of Purebred Dogs* (by Clark and Stainer)
❏ General health medications, such as Pepto-Bismol® and aspirin

Security/Emergency Equipment

Though this is the chapter's shortest list, it's among the most important.

❏ Padlocks, preferably keyed alike, for securing runs and yard gates when you have to be away for a time

❏ Smoke alarms that are loud enough for you to hear them from inside your house

❏ Charged fire extinguishers, along with practiced knowledge about their proper use

❏ A list of emergency phone numbers: doctors (MDs as well as DVMs), hospitals, ambulance services, fire departments and law enforcement agencies. Make several copies of this list and post them in various locations in your kennel and your home. Keep one in your pocket, too.

Miscellaneous equipment, in this case an intercom locked open so indoor kennel activity can be monitored from another location (such as the house), a smoke alarm and ear protectors.

Grooming Supplies

If you don't offer complete grooming services, the following essentials should be adequate.

- Brushes of various types
- Combs of various types
- Grooming table
- Hair dryer
- Dematting tools
- Nail clippers of various sizes
- Rinses
- Stripping combs of various sizes
- Shampoos

Cleaning Supplies

The following is a list of the bare essentials you should have on hand. Some facilities will need additional items, such as a vacuum cleaner for indoor/outdoor carpeting.

- Brooms
- Buckets
- Disinfectants
- Feces scoops
- Fly strips
- Fly swatters
- Hoses and nozzles. The hoses should be able to handle hot water without disintegrating internally, as regular hoses may. But don't use a hot-water hose for filling dogs' water buckets, regardless of water temperature; water that has been in contact with a hot-water hose's lining can cause diarrhea.
- Laundry baskets
- Mops
- Paper towels
- Rubber kitchen gloves
- Scrub brushes
- Snow shovels (if necessary)
- Soaps (hand soap and laundry soap as needed)
- Sponges
- Spray bottles (plastic, not glass)
- Squeegees
- Waste baskets
- All-purpose household cleaner

Two types of squeegees. The larger of the two—which measures 24 inches wide—is more useful on outdoor runs. Squeegees can also be used for latching hard-to-reach windows.

Maintenance Tools

As with all physical structures, some amount of maintenance is necessary under ordinary wear and tear. And as your business grows and matures, you may find that you need to add or change your original setup. Keep a basic set of tools on hand, and you'll be prepared no matter what happens when:

❑ A spool of electric-fence wire, which can be great for tightening or reattaching stretched or bent chainlink.
❑ Drill
❑ Duct tape
❑ Hammer
❑ Heavy-duty wire cutters
❑ Inside-drain plugs
❑ Ladders that can safely reach your kennel's roof
❑ Measuring tape
❑ Nut drivers
❑ Pliers
❑ Plunger
❑ Plumber's snake
❑ Screwdrivers (flat-blade and Phillips) of various sizes
❑ Stepladders
❑ Tin snips
❑ Trowel (for patching and repairing concrete)
❑ Wrenches of various sizes

If you do decide to make an office part of your kennel, spoil yourself. This kenneler obviously did.

Office Equipment and Supplies

Regardless of whether you maintain an office in your kennel, you'll need some basic equipment and supplies to handle daily operations and bookkeeping.

- ❑ Calculator
- ❑ Lockable box for cash and checks
- ❑ Pens and pencils
- ❑ Permanent markers
- ❑ Paper
- ❑ Clipboards
- ❑ Index cards
- ❑ Stapler
- ❑ Staple remover
- ❑ Paper clips
- ❑ Scissors
- ❑ Ruler
- ❑ Clock
- ❑ Calendar
- ❑ Filing cabinet
- ❑ File folders
- ❑ At least a one-month supply of all forms you use

Miscellaneous Equipment and Supplies

You might think that the preceding lists must surely have told you everything you need to have, but they don't quite do it. Here are some additional things that would be good to have on hand.

- ❏ Two flashlights and spare batteries and bulbs
- ❏ Extra light bulbs
- ❏ Extra batteries for equipment that uses batteries (especially smoke detectors)
- ❏ A radio with an automatic shut-off feature, set to a station offering restful music. Avoid screeching, God's-gonna-get-you preachers, heavy rock music and debate programming, as such noises can make dogs nervous.
- ❏ Blankets and terrycloth towels for dogs to rest upon (but don't use these with chewers, as ingestion of cloth can be fatal).
- ❏ Washable leash-and-collar containers for storing owners' equipment. One container per run, numbered to correspond with each run.
- ❏ Cages for housing destructive dogs
- ❏ Welder's gloves for handling small aggressive or fearful dogs
- ❏ A heavy coat you can quickly don that is capable of minimizing low-intensity bites or scratches that can occur when dealing with large, aggressive or fearful dogs.
- ❏ A noose-and-pole restraint
- ❏ Small fans for circulating air
- ❏ Large fans for drying runs
- ❏ Heavy-duty extension cords
- ❏ Room thermometers
- ❏ Ear protectors (for you, not the dogs)
- ❏ Waterproof boots
- ❏ Umbrella, which is especially useful when receiving or returning dogs during a rainstorm
- ❏ Leashes and collars

A Wall-Mounted Scheduler

Although I have all the details of my boarders on record, I find it helpful to have an entire week's schedule posted where I can easily see it. I use a dry-erase board and markers for recording each dog's name, the brand of food he is to be fed, the frequency of feedings and the food-bowl and water-bucket identification numbers. You might prefer to use a chalkboard, a wet-erase board or one of those laminated-plastic, erasable schedulers you can purchase at office supply stores.

Because some of the information never changes, I actually used a permanent marker to write on my dry-erase board. See the figure on page 101 for the headings I use.

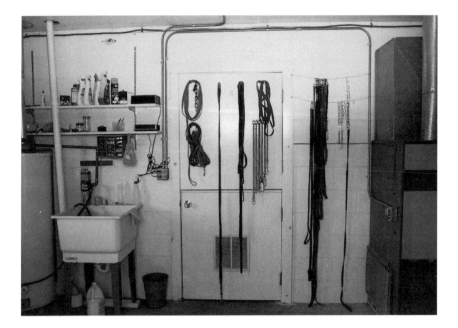

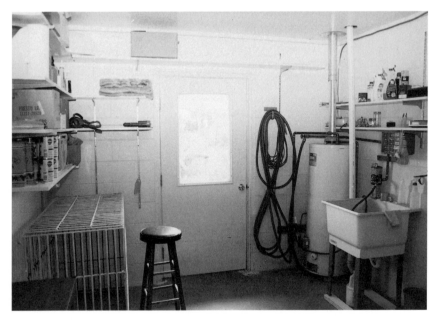

Two views of a kennel's storeroom.

Current Boarders

Run #	Dog's Name	Food Type	AM (Qty)	Noon (Qty)	PM (Qty)	Bowl	Water	Notes
1								
2								
3								

For the information that changes day to day (or dog to dog), I use the regular dry-erase markers—dog's name, brand of food, amounts to feed, food-bowl and water-bucket numbers. The headings AM (Qty), Noon (Qty) and PM (Qty) refer to cups of kibble (or cans or fractions) per feeding.

The headings Bowl and Water refer to the identification number for each container, the idea being to lessen the chance of inadvertently switching one animal's food bowl or water bucket with another's. The Notes column is for recording medication frequency and dosages and other uncommon information. Update the transitory information as each boarder arrives and erase it when she departs.

#	NAME	FOOD	AM	N	PM	DISH	H₂O	OTHER-	L
1									
2	MOXEY	EM	1¼	–	1¼	16			
3									
4	PUPPY	EM	2	–	2	21			
5	HONEY & KISSES	EM	½	–	½	7			
6	TEDDY	own	½	–	½	6			
7	Brigette	EM	1½	–	1½	3			
8	DUDLEY	EM	2	–	2	14			
9	COCOA	EM	1	–	1	17			
10	ERIN – RAISA DR	EM	1½	–	1½	20			

A board such as this can have many uses in a boarding kennel.

A three-by-five card attached to each interior run gate, showing the boarder's name and veterinarian, provides essential information at a glance.

Telephone Equipment and Services

Communication is the key to connecting with your customers, and depending on the size of your business you may need more than just a plain-old home telephone and telephone line.

Cordless Phone

If you don't have a phone line in your kennel—and even if you do—it might be wise to invest in a cordless phone that you can answer wherever you are in the kennel. Also, when I need to contact a vet, I don't want to be hampered by cords while describing a dog's condition, and my cordless phone solves that problem.

Answering Machine or Service

I know people who still resist getting a telephone-answering machine or service, but no business should be without one or the other. Machines are so inexpensive these days that one single message that results in a booking can pay for it. Your answering message should never be cold and unfriendly, but keep it brief, businesslike and to the point. A long message or one with idiotic sound effects will lose many a caller, as many people don't have the patience to sit through a rambling, infantile or hard-on-the-ears recording.

Most phone companies these days provide a voice-messaging service for their customers for a fee. If you don't want to invest in an answering machine, this type of service might be a feasible alternative.

Call-Waiting

You might want to consider adding call-waiting to your existing telephone service, either as an alternative to an answering machine or service or in addition to it. If your personal phone and business phone are the same, as is the case at many small-business operations, call-waiting lets you know during a call that you have another incoming call. Although the service isn't free, it can result in a booking (and income) that you might otherwise miss.

A Second Line for Business

Is your home phone adequate for serving your business needs, or do you need some sort of separate telephone service? If you have teenagers, or if there are other reasons why your home phone might often be busy, the increased cost of a separate business line might be money well spent. Customers don't like having to fight with a perpetual busy signal, and they may decide to solve the problem by calling elsewhere.

You really have a few options here. You could have a second physical phone line installed to be used strictly for your kenneling business, but you should be aware that telephone companies always charge more for business service than for residential lines.

You could purchase a cellular phone and calling package. You would still have the additional expense of a separate line, but you would have a built-in cordless phone as part of the deal. Another alternative would be a pager, which may be the least expensive option for additional service; the downside to a pager, though, is that it's less convenient. Although the caller can find you anytime, anywhere, you need to find your way to a telephone to call them back.

I can make a legitimate case for having either a cellular phone or a pager—your kennel helpers should always be able to reach you when you're away from the property. At the same time, when I have a rare evening out with friends, I don't really want to discuss reservations with a client. That's why I have an answering machine instead. Moral: You may be wise to have a pager and/or a cell phone, but you may be even wiser to limit the number of people who have the numbers.

Motion Sensors and Intercoms

A motion sensor in the supply room, connected to an alarm in your home, is peace-of-mind equipment for detecting intruders or a dog who has managed to escape from a run. Similarly, an intercom unit locked open in the kennels and connected to a receiver in your house is useful for monitoring routine activity without disturbing the occupants.

Sunscreens

Depending on your climate and the amount of nearby tree shade, you may want to acquire a few rolls of sunscreen material for attaching across the tops and last-panel sides of outdoor runs. Available in various styles and colors, the material is lightweight, inexpensive, durable and easy to install. If you live in the snowbelt, don't leave sunscreens attached to your runs during winter. The weight of accumulated snow—especially the wet, large-flake variety—can collapse the runs.

Lightweight and easy to install, sunscreens can markedly lower outdoor run temperatures.

The plastic material is easily attached with electric-fence wire to an outdoor-run gate.

Run Guards

This plastic material is often used as kitchen-runner strip surfacing and is commonly available in 1-foot widths. When attached horizontally to outdoor run gates and flush with the concrete, this material deflects substances into the clean-out trough—instead of the walkway—as you are hosing down the run.

Nightly Checklist

Prior to shutting down the kennels every night, it's a good idea to work from a written checklist to verify that all your chores have been done and the kennel is secure. It's way too easy to overlook something you know so well that you've forgotten you know it, especially if it's a routine chore at day's end when you're tired.

- ❑ Are all dogs inside?
- ❑ Does each dog appear healthy?
- ❑ Has all medication been dispensed?
- ❑ Exterior doors locked?
- ❑ Perimeter gates locked?

- ❑ All run-access doors closed?
- ❑ Windows opened or closed, as needed?
- ❑ Storeroom's interior-access door closed?
- ❑ Food containers closed?
- ❑ All water turned off at the source?
- ❑ Radio set to switch off in half an hour?
- ❑ Security system on?
- ❑ Intercom on?
- ❑ Heat set for the right temperature?
- ❑ Has everyone been petted today?
- ❑ Has everyone had a good-night biscuit?

Reflection

Be prepared.

MOTTO OF THE BOY SCOUTS OF AMERICA

Daily Operations

Establishing a routine and maintaining records are essential for running a business. In this chapter, I explain the process that I follow at my kennel and also show you examples of the forms I use. The forms are provided generically, since you may see ways to customize them for your business.

Reservations

The first time a client calls to reserve space, I fill out a Boarding Reservation Form. This document gives me a starting point in my records of each boarder's history.

Of course, you also need to schedule the appointment. You should keep an appointment book of some sort so you can see who's coming and going when. I use the Available Boarding Space form shown here.

I copy the client's last name from the Boarding Reservation form onto the line corresponding to the arrival date. I enter the planned arrival time in that block's upper-right corner. Anytime I board more than one dog per run, I record the number of dogs in the block's upper-left corner. I draw a line through the dates the customer is reserving and note the anticipated departure time in the upper-right corner of the last block needed. A sample entry appears above for a client named

Boarding Reservation

Owner: _____ Phone #: _____ Today's Date: _____

Date In: _____ Time: _____ Date Out: _____ Time: _____

	Breed	Name	Age	Sex
#1				
#2				
#3				
#4				

Number of Dogs per Run: _____

Vaccinations: ☐ Rabies ☐ Distemper ☐ Parvo-Virus
☐ Corona ☐ Kennel Cough ☐ Other: _____

Veterinarian: _____

Notes: _____

_____

Available Boarding Space

Month of _____ Year _____

Day	Run 1	Run 2	Run 3	Run 4	Run 5	Run 6	
1							
2							
3	2Jones9AM						
4							
5							
6							
7	2Jones6PM						
8							

Jones whose two dogs need one run, and who will arrive on the third of the month at 9:00 AM and depart on the seventh at 6:00 PM.

With run numbers across the top and dates down the left side, this form lets you look ahead and back. You can see at a glance who is coming and going on any given date, as well as your run availability. The form is also useful for reviewing past business periods. Of course, more than one sheet per month may be necessary, depending on your number of runs.

If all your runs are the same size, allocate them in numerical sequence whenever possible, using the columns in left-to-right fashion. This makes it easy to see how much space is available for any given date. That is, unless your runs are of different sizes or appointments, you need not assign specific run numbers when reservations are made. Recording a client's name under run number nine, for example, doesn't mean that his dog will occupy that particular run. The purpose here is to account for the *number* of runs reserved for given dates, not to assign specific runs.

If you sometimes rent runs twice during the same day, either increase the size of the squares when preparing the form or plan on writing in small print occasionally.

For dogs whose stays extend into the next month, maintain continuity with a down arrow ($\downarrow$) in the run column after the last day of the month, and enter the planned departure date next to the arrow. Enter the names of clients whose pets are carryovers from the prior month on the first line of the new month's Available Boarding Space form, showing an up arrow ($\uparrow$) for the arrival date.

After making your entry on the Available Boarding Space form, file the Boarding Reservation form according to arrival date.

If you prefer, skip the first step of completing a Boarding Reservation form when dealing with established clientele. Because such information as the dog's name, vet's name and so forth is already on file, you can enter the requested arrival and departure dates and times directly onto the Available Boarding Space sheet.

Dogs Who Hurt People

They're out there. Every so often someone will call and tell me about their bad-tempered whatever and, "Sometimes he nips, heh heh heh." Think, "Not me, he doesn't," and translate the caller's comment into "That dog will bite anything that moves." Without being rude, turn down the business, perhaps referring the caller to another local boarding-kennel operator, one whom you don't particularly like.

Arrivals

Having an established routine for arriving animals—and their people—will make your life a lot easier, not to mention making a good impression on your clients.

On-Leash, Please

Insist that all dogs arrive and depart on-leash. Further, take pooch's leash from the owner as they enter your main gate or office. In some states you are legally responsible for the animal the moment he sets foot on your property, so take control of his actions quickly. (Keep a few leashes and collars handy for instances when clients tell you, "I forgot my leash and collar at home.") Besides, landscaping is expensive, and you don't need dogs to hoist a leg on a tree. Not only is that rough on the tree, but it can also transmit disease to other dogs who sniff an afflicted animal's leavings.

As you take the leash, close the main gate to prevent flight should a leash or collar separate. Then ask the owner to wait while you take the dog to a run. If the owner asks to accompany you, honor the request.

A Quick General Exam

Make a cursory examination of every dog upon arrival. Check for limping, hair loss, runny or glazed eyes, labored breathing or a persistent, dry, hacking cough. Should you observe any of these signs, or any others you consider abnormal, stop right then and there and bring the matter to the owner's attention. Should he be unable to explain the condition satisfactorily, refer him to a veterinarian before boarding the animal. You are within your rights to do so; furthermore, it's your responsibility to protect the dog as well as those animals already in your care.

If you handle a dog you suspect of illness, scrub your hands with antibacterial soap before going near other dogs. If the animal coughs on you, change your clothes. Some germs can survive on clothing for days.

Housing Assignments

Because dark-coated animals absorb more heat, house them on your kennel's shady side. Also, if one area of your facility is cooler than others, that's where to put the "Northern Lights" breeds (Siberian Huskies, Alaskan Malamutes, Samoyeds, and so on).

When you board playful, vocal dogs, especially those owned by the same person and housed in separate runs, put some distance between them to maintain a quiet kennel at night. If you put those dogs next to each other, they are less likely to be calm. Granted, just two dogs woofing at one another isn't a great problem, but their antics may ignite other boarders.

Acclimating a New Boarder

Place each new arrival in the outside section of his assigned run, keeping the door to the inside run closed to prevent entry for now. The combination of travel and being in a new place often stimulates a dog to eliminate, and it is preferable that he see from the get-go that some things are better done outside than inside.

A Word of Caution

There should be nothing in any run that a dog could catch his collar on. In deference to Murphy's Law, however, and the fact that a dog can jam a rear foot under a collar when scratching an itch about his neck, always remove each dog's collar once you have him in his run. Then you're certain he can't catch his collar on anything.

Canine Comfort

If a dog seems nervous in his new surroundings, spend a few minutes petting and talking to him, keeping your message an upbeat "I'm really glad you're here!" not "It's all right, don't worry." As mentioned earlier, reassurance often deepens a nervous dog's anxiety. It's better to give the animal the opportunity to imitate your optimistic attitude. Sure, this takes time and causes new clients to have to await your return to complete paperwork (established ones can depart as soon as you take their dogs), but they'll keep. The dog's emotional well-being is your main concern.

Similarly, after removing a dog's collar, should he trot away to check out the other boarders and investigate his new digs, leave the run without further ado. The critter is demonstrating that his mental and emotional states are fine and that he wants to explore on his own. Your continued presence at this point can only complicate matters.

Equipment Storage

Once you've left a new arrival in a run, place his leash and collar in an indoor container numbered to correspond with the run. This ensures that the owner won't inadvertently forget the equipment at home when he comes to pick up pooch.

Another line of thinking goes like this: Because owners can arrive with pooch's collar so loose that the animal could pull his head out of it, some boarding-kennel operators prefer to attach their own leash and collar upon arrival. The owner's leash and collar aren't kept at the kennel, because the kennel operator also uses his own equipment during departures. That's all well and good, and I greet all arrivals with an adjustable collar and leash in my pocket in case a collar or leash appears loose or frayed; but I still prefer to retain the owner's equipment to be sure he'll have a means for controlling the animal when they arrive home. True, in theory the dog is not my problem once he leaves my premises, but we all know the value of applying theories to practical matters. By making certain that each owner arrives home with equipment for controlling his pet, I sleep better.

Boarding Record and Boarding Contract

Though completing paperwork may be the first step at your facility, I don't maintain an office per se, preferring to meet each new arrival at my gate so that if a sick dog arrives I can stop things immediately, not after the animal has set foot (and possibly disease) in my kennels.

After housing the dog, I grab a clipboard holding all necessary forms and return to the owner to start a client/pet history by filling out the following Boarding Record form. In the event that the owner boards more than one dog, I complete a Boarding Record form for each animal. True, much of the information will be the same for each dog from a particular household, but by having a record for each dog, I avoid confusion when the owner subsequently does not board all of his pets with me or when he no longer has some of them.

Vaccinations	The dates of current vaccinations.
Food	Kennel's or owner's: Who provides the food?
Date/Time In	When you received the dog.
Date/Time Out	When the dog departed.
Collar	How many and what kind of collar(s) the dog wears.
Leash	The owner's type and color of leash.
Bed	Bedding the owner provided, described as "green blanket," "gray cedar pillow," and so on.
Food	Brand and quantity of food the owner provided.

Kennel Name
City and State
Boarding Record

| Owner | | Dog's Call Name |

| Address | | Breed |

| | | at | | |
| City, State, Zip | | Age | Date | Sex | Alt |

| Telephone | Email | Veterinarian |

Medical Problems, Allergies, etc.

Vaccinations: ☐ Rabies ☐ Distemper ☐ Parvo-Virus
☐ Corona ☐ Kennel Cough ☐ Other: _____

Food: Kennel's _____ Amount per Feeding (cups):

Owner's _____ AM ____ N ____ PM ____ E ____

IN Date/Time	OUT Date/Time	Collar	Leash	Bed	Food	Rx	Other	Charges

Boarding Notes: _____

_____

_____

_____

_____

_____

_____

_____

Rx	Quantity and types of medications the owner provided.
Other	Miscellaneous items the owner provided.
Charges	How much the owner spent with you for this visit; enter this amount after the dog is picked up.

Next, have the owner sign your Boarding Contract, a sample of which follows, and provide him or her with a copy of the document. If an owner boards several pets, protect yourself legally by getting a separate signed contract for each animal.

As you can see, the dog is not specifically identified by name, breed or other criteria. This is because I print the document on the reverse side of the Boarding Record form, making further identification of the animal unnecessary. This not only centralizes all data for each dog, but also means I have half as many pieces of paper. If you prefer to designate the animal, simply add a line reading "Dog's Name" at the top of the document.

Also notice that the dog is referred to as a "pet." The idea behind such wording, instead of the more vague terminology "dog," is to lessen the odds of a massive lawsuit should a tragedy befall the creature while in your care, and the owner claiming in court that the animal was a "show dog" of great value.

Last, note that you need to execute this contract just once—at the dog's first visit. That's the intent of the contract's final paragraph: to reduce paperwork, eliminate folderol and let established clients be on their way as quickly as possible.

Computer Users

If you have computerized your records, you can eliminate the Boarding Record form by entering the information directly into your computer. The Boarding Contract text still must be printed for the owner to sign, which means you have to add a line to the contract for printing the owner's name since signatures aren't always legible.

Goodbye, Hello

Owners influence a boarded dog's mental state. I've seen people wave and call to their pets as they depart and when they return. Using the animal's name, they sing out *"Auf Wiedersehen"* or *"We're back!"*

Kennel Name

Address

City, State, Zip Code

BOARDING CONTRACT

This is a Contract between [*Kennel Name*] and the pet Owner.

Kennel agrees to exercise due and reasonable care, and to keep the kennel premises sanitary and properly enclosed.

The dog(s) is to be fed properly and regularly, and to be housed in clean, safe quarters.

All dogs are boarded or are otherwise handled or cared for by Kennel without liability on Kennel's part for loss or damage from disease, theft, fire, death, running away, injury, or harm to persons, other dogs, or property by said dog, or other unavoidable causes, due diligence and care having been exercised.

Owner agrees to pay to Kennel [*rate, in numbers*] ([*rate, in words*]) per pet per day for boarding service.
Owner understands and agrees that dog(s) picked up by Owner after 1:00PM shall be charged for an additional full day's stay.

All charges incurred by Owner shall be payable upon pick-up of pet(s).

Owner further agrees that pet(s) shall not leave the Kennel until all charges are paid to Kennel by Owner.

Kennel shall have, and is hereby granted, a lien on the pet(s) for any and all unpaid charges resulting from boarding pet(s) at Kennel.

If the pet(s) becomes ill or if the state of the animal's health otherwise requires professional attention, Kennel, in its sole discretion, may engage the services of a veterinarian of its choosing, administer medicine or give other requisite attention to the animal, and expenses thereof shall be paid by Owner.

It is understood by Kennel and Owner that all provisions of this Contract shall be binding upon both parties thereunto for this visit and for all subsequent visits. This Contract contains the entire agreement between the parties.

_____   _____
Owner   *Date*

_____   _____
Kennel   *Date*

But those intended messages and the ones the dog actually receives are often different. In people terms, goodbyes and hellos signify partings and greetings. To a confined dog, an owner calling to him from afar is anxiety-producing, especially in the case of goodbyes. The dog has no earthly notion why his people have left him. He just knows that he is there and that his family is not. Nor can he foresee that his owner will return for him. This is especially true of first-time boarders.

Many owners are unfamiliar with such concepts, having never realized a dog's perception differs from ours. But most will understand when you explain, and that will benefit everyone concerned; the owner will become more knowledgeable about his pet, the dog will be more settled and you won't have an upset boarder.

Something for Pooch

Even if you spend time with the animal upon arrival, after the owners depart spend a few more minutes with their dog. Make a friend. The creature may be in something of a vulnerable state emotionally, having just watched his people leave, and it's a good time for you to take their place insofar as letting him know that you like him and can be trusted. It's also an opportunity for you to get a reading on temperament and predispositions, which is information you need.

After visiting with the dog for a bit, open his inside/outside run-access door, slowly with new boarders, quickly with practiced ones. A new boarder may not realize that this is a door and the sound and quick motion of a guillotine door can startle him. Seasoned boarders know the routine and may bump their heads rushing inside if you open the door slowly.

Next, place a bucket of cool, clean water in the indoor run. Make sure the dog sees you do this; he may view it as the act of a friend because it is reminiscent of something his family does for him.† Placing the water bucket in the inside run also serves to designate that area as "home" or "nest," suggesting that it isn't to be fouled. A fresh capful of the product ReaLemon® added to a dog's drinking water can decrease the odds that he'll suffer an attack of the trots caused by differences between his house's water chemistry and yours.

---

†Should the dog have aggressive or extreme territorial tendencies, protect yourself by placing the bucket in the indoor run prior to opening the inside/outside run-access door, or when he is outside and near the run's far end.

Keeping Track of Who's Who

Attached to the top bar of each inside run gate is a clip into which I insert a three-by-five card showing the names of the dog, the owner and his veterinarian. It isn't just helpful in getting to know new boarders; it can save time in an emergency.

Departures

Before you turn a dog back over to his owner, you should take care of all the paperwork and payment business.

Checkout Time

Hotels charge for a full day if guests don't check out by a certain hour. Given the conceptual similarities between hotels and boarding kennels, I follow the same principle; my checkout time is 1:00 PM.

Some clients think 24 hours should constitute a boarding day, and in their place we might see it similarly. Thus I explain to those who ask, "Owners often drop their dogs off in the morning, so if I let boarders stay much past the lunch hour at no charge I'd likely have to turn down another client." Most come to see and understand my position.

Does this mean I will zing a customer for a full day's boarding should he pick up his dog at 1:08 in the afternoon? Of course not. If we are discussing a frequent boarder, I would even stretch the checkout time by an hour or so as long as I don't have to turn away business to do so. What if it's a slow time of year and the client, whose dog has been with you for three weeks, shows up at 2:20? Do you assess another day's boarding? I wouldn't, but I'd make sure the owner knows he's getting a break: "Checkout time's one o'clock, but it's not a problem today."

Now, this policy can raise questions. What if a dog arrives at 8:00 AM and departs around noon on the same day? Or what if he leaves at 2:00 PM on the same day? Or 4:00 PM? My answer for all three scenarios would be the same: charge for a half day. It's likely that I'll be able to rent that run that evening.

What if the dog arrives at 9:00 PM on, say, Monday, and leaves at 7:00 PM on Tuesday? That's less than a 24-hour stay, true, but I would charge for two days if I had to turn down other Tuesday-arrival business for the dog to stay until seven o'clock that evening.

Remember that each situation is unique. Did an emergency force the owner's return or the trip itself? If so, you might do well to show a little compassion. In the case of the dog who will depart at 7:00 PM, can you talk another client into bringing his pet to you at 7:30 PM (giving you time to clean the run) instead of at 6:30 PM, as he'd requested? If so, or if you can cage the new arrival or put him in an exercise yard for an hour, there's no need to charge the first owner for a second day's stay.

Remember: Inflexible policies can hurt a business long-term, and long-term is what you care about. With a checkout time of 1:00 PM, you're not trying to gouge people. That's not the idea at all. You're trying to avoid losing revenue you would have otherwise earned for the day when a dog that stayed with you the previous night goes home late in the day.

Settle the Account First

A small point of procedure pertains to settling the account, specifically "When?" When a client arrives to pick up his best friend, I report the amount due and ask him to prepare a check while I get pooch. To first-time boarders I explain, "It's just easier to get your paperwork out of the way before you and your pal are reunited. This way, you can give him your full attention when we return." I've never had anyone respond with, "Let me see my dog first," probably because at that point I've only asked that they write their check, not give it to me.

Cash or Charge?

I accept local checks or cash. Whether you should take credit cards is your decision. I don't take plastic because it's time-consuming and because doing so would increase my costs. To my knowledge, I've never lost a client over the issue.

A related consideration is whether to offer personal charge accounts. At my kennels it's "cash-and-carry," and I explain to the few who have asked that I don't want to get into the extra bookkeeping. Again, I've yet to lose any business over this policy.

For customers paying in cash, it's a good idea to keep some money on hand, paper and coins, for making change.

Receipts

Though several types of receipt blanks are available commercially, computer users can cut that expense by creating and printing their own. A sample receipt form follows.

Kennel Name			Receipt #: _____
Received From: _____			Date: _____
Amount: _____			Dollars

Account Balance	$
This Payment	$
Balance Due	$

Payment For: _____

_____

Received By: _____

Receipt #	Used if you sequentially number your receipts. I don't, mainly because clients seldom request one, knowing that their canceled check is a receipt, and because receipt numbers aren't essential to my bookkeeping system.
Received From	The client making the payment.
Date	The date you received the payment.
Amount...Dollars	The amount of the payment in words.
Account Balance	The amount the client owed before this payment.
This Payment	The amount of this payment in numbers.
Balance Due	Account Balance minus This Payment.
Payment For	The service or product you sold; for example, "Boarding—Old Buster."
Received By	The signature of the person receiving the payment.

Bye-Bye

While this is perhaps an unnecessary suggestion, after reuniting the dog with the owner, pet the animal and say his name just before they leave. Sure, owners like to see this, but more important is the fact that the dog has been in your care for a time; he's probably gotten to like you, and a little pat of attention just before he leaves will say good things to him about your appreciation of him. It's akin to the training notion of always ending a session on a positive note, praising the dog for correct behavior. It makes the dog's next visit with you that much easier and nicer for him. Besides, it's fun for you.

Reflection

I'm really innocent—I only look guilty.

CAPTION ON A POSTER DEPICTING A
WORRIED-LOOKING DACHSHUND PUPPY

Policies and Practices

Client Issues

Don't Sublet

Let's say it's one of those delightful times when your kennel is booked to capacity. A valued client calls to ask if you have space for Old Buster. You don't, but you know Old B to be a gentle animal and that another boarder of similar disposition and good health is already in house. You believe that neither dog would fight for any reason. Do you let them share a run?

No.

Let's make it trickier. What if Old Buster's owners and those of the other dog—we'll call him Clyde—are next-door neighbors, and Old B and Clyde are buddies who have played together since puppyhood? Now may they share a run?

No.

What if the caller says, "Look, I know Clyde is there with you. He and Old Buster get along great. How about putting them in together? It's certainly okay with me."

No. Not without the permission—and here's the key—of *both* owners. To put Old B in with any dog without both owners' consent, or to put one dog in an inside run and another in the outside section while keeping the run-access door closed, effactually separating them, not only is ethically wrong, but also violates stipulations in the boarding contract. Specifically, the

121

phrases, "due and reasonable care," "the dog is to be . . . housed in . . . safe quarters," and "due diligence and care having been exercised."

Perhaps a kenneler might think, "I could take Old Buster if I'd stick that Cocker who's in run number six in an airline crate for a few days." That would work, but don't do it. The Cocker's owner is paying for a run, not a cage, and while I might cage a dog for a short time (like a half an hour or so) to free a run, it's chintzy to meaningfully deprive an animal of proper housing just to sweeten the day's take.

Can Old Buster's owner be accommodated? That depends on whether another dog will be leaving soon. Then I'd be willing to keep a dog like Old B in my house until a run opens, and have often done so for valued owners of well-mannered pets. During one hectic Christmas, in fact, I gave a client's German Shepherd free run of my home and allowed her to sleep on my bed for three nights until a run became available. (The only problem then was that she didn't think much of going into a run.) Often an ethical way can be found to accommodate steady customers during peak times without shortchanging other boarders.

Allowing Dogs to Socialize

Would I let Old Buster and Clyde play together, under supervision, in an exercise yard? Only if both owners approve. If either owner isn't comfortable with the idea, I won't allow the dogs to be together for any reason.

Giving Every Dog His Due

I doubt that every kennel owner is crazy about every dog they board. Most of them, yes, but some others bring into our days all the joys of an impacted wisdom tooth. Should you find yourself in a situation like the one described earlier—needing but not having a run for the nice dog of a good client—would it occur to you to stick a bad-tempered critter you don't particularly like into a cage for a few days so you can take Old B? Such thoughts have crossed my mind, but that's as far as I let them go. That animal occupying the run in which I'd like to put Old B may not be much of a dog in my estimation, but she was brought to me because her owner felt her pet would receive the best care I could provide, and several days of caging doesn't qualify.

Intentional Overbooking

Kennels sometimes accept more reservations than they can handle to cover themselves against no-shows or last-minute cancellations. The number of runs by which they overbook is commonly determined by seasonal factors and percentage formulas. While the idea may have merit at very large operations, it's a fool's game for a small kennel. The question becomes not *will* you eventually have a problem of more dogs than runs, but *when* will you have a problem of more dogs than runs.

Clients with Unusual Conditions or Needs

Over the years a few callers have informed me that their dogs had not and would not receive traditional vaccinations because they didn't believe in preventative medicine. I declined their business and suggest you do the same. To do otherwise is to endanger your other boarders. Boarders at my kennels must be currently vaccinated against distemper, leptospirosis, hepatitis, parvo, rabies, corona and tracheobronchitis (kennel cough). If at any time you doubt a client's honesty, request written certification, signed by a veterinarian, attesting that the dog's shots are current.

Callers have wanted to board their pets as early as 5:00 AM. After pointing out that I'm open from 7:00 AM until 10:00 PM, seven days a week, most were content to arrive at a more reasonable hour. A minority made arrangements elsewhere, which was probably just as well.

Understand, I've taken dogs at all hours when clients faced emergencies. That's an obligation I feel toward my customers. But to routinely accept reservations for arrival while the roosters are still comatose not only upsets the patterns of current boarders, but makes my day too long as well.

Incidentally, the policy of releasing pets as late as ten o'clock at night provides a significant edge on the competition. When people return from a trip they want their pets, and while they'll abide a policy of "We close at five," they don't like it. They put up with it because they have no choice. The problem is compounded when the owners must work the day after their return and—because they can't get their dogs until afterward—are charged for another day's boarding. Offering late pickups increases goodwill and decreases your load the following morning.

Keep a List of Troublesome Clients

It's common sense to keep at least a mental list of your better clients. But how about those whose business you are better off without? For purposes of organization, my *No-No* roster has three categories: no-shows, bad checks and chronic complainers.

No-shows honor maybe half the reservations they make. They not only don't arrive, they seldom let me know they aren't coming. *Bad checks* are self-explanatory. Someone who writes me one "NSF" (Non-Sufficient

Funds) check doesn't get put on this list—accidents can happen—but a second rubber check constitutes automatic induction into my hall of infamy.

Chronic complainers are those whom nothing pleases. Of course, if a client has criticisms or complaints, I want to know about them. Customers can see things that you and I might miss—our closeness to the operation can distort our perspective—and I appreciate it when someone takes the time to point out something they think could be improved. Habitual whiners, however, are another story. They gripe when they arrive, gripe again when they collect their pet and probably complain during their entire trip. I've had a few such clients, and in each case all my runs were booked when they next called for reservations, if you take my meaning. I follow the same policy with *No-shows* and *Bad-check* writers.

Respect the Privacy of Clients

It may happen that a caller will ask, "Are you boarding the Smith's dog right now?" The answer to that question is, "I'm sorry, but I can't give out that information."

Sure, the question's basis is probably innocent, but perhaps the caller intends evil doings, like burglarizing the Smith residence, and is trying to verify that they are indeed away from home.

A similar situation can go like this.

"I'm here to pick up the Smith's dog."

"Who are you?"

"I'm Jane Jones, the Smith's neighbor."

"I'm sorry, Ms. Jones, but if the Smith's dog is indeed here I can release her only to the owner. It has to do with protecting clients and their pets and maintaining confidentiality, don't you see."

Again, perhaps there's no problem here. Maybe the person is who she says she is, and maybe the Smiths did ask her to collect their pet. However, unless the client has made advance arrangements, you may not only be putting the dog at risk, but also could be placing yourself in legal jeopardy by acknowledging that the animal is at your facility or by releasing her to anyone but the owner without authorization.

Make a point of asking clients, especially new ones, "Will you be coming to pick up your pet yourself?" If the spouse of a new client will be picking up the animal, advise your customer that he or she must bring identification for you to release the dog.

Handling Premature Departures

A situation you'll face pertains to clients who return earlier than planned. They book a run for a week, for example, but return after five days. So, do you charge them for the time reserved—seven days—or for the five days actually used? Or do you split the difference at six days rental?

I charge clients for time used, irrespective of what was booked. I want to see the client again, and we all know what it's like to be nickeled and dimed. We also know how such experiences left us with a bad taste, resolving to trade elsewhere next time. Boarding kennel clients are no different. Trying to charge for time unused can incur bad will. A few good people have offered to pay for the time reserved, but I declined their money because I'm not comfortable with being paid for something I haven't done.

Kennel Inspections by Clients

Why not? Every so often a caller will ask to look over my facilities prior to making a reservation, and I'm happy to provide a tour and answer questions. It also provides an opportunity to complete initial paperwork prior to the dog's actual first visit. When I schedule such appointments, I ask callers to bring their dog with them (so I can assess temperament) but to leave her in their car while we tour the kennels. A strange dog wandering about the place can upset boarders already in house.

Dog Issues
Cover Thine, and the Dog's

I wrote in *Dog Logic—Companion Obedience,* "Don't acquire a canine you can't easily control physically in any situation when the animal is full grown." The same principle applies to boarding kennel operators: Don't take any dog you cannot handle physically in a high-stress situation. To do otherwise is to put yourself at risk from aggressive dogs, and can also endanger the dog. How? Let's say you have an emergency requiring immediate veterinary attention—you *must* get a boarder to a vet right away. Now let's make that dog about 180 pounds worth of unconscious St. Bernard. Can you get that much dead weight over to and into your vehicle? What if the animal were conscious but delirious? Could you control her sufficiently to get her to a DVM? If the answer to any question is no, should you board such an animal in the first place?

Females in Season

The question is whether to board them. My policy is not to. A host of chemicals for knocking down odor is available, but the canine nose is keen, and any mask is only so effective. Dogs soon learn a lady is about, and the incidence of fence fighting becomes greater and more intense. The charged atmosphere inflicts too much stress on everyone, including the female.

Puppies

Should you board them? I suppose it comes down to "What's a puppy?" I won't take any dog not fully immunized. Since puppies must receive an initial series of shots, I decline to take any with incomplete vaccinations.

When to Take a Boarder to the Vet

I tell owners who ask, "About all a dog has to do is look at me cross-eyed and I'm taking her to a vet." Seriously, I have to see a bit more symptomatology than that before bundling a dog off to the good doctor, but not too much more. Remember: I'm not a veterinarian. I don't know every aspect of each boarder's medical history, nor do I consider myself an expert on every health nuance peculiar to every breed. My two guidelines are simple:

- What would I want someone to do for my dog?
- If in doubt, call a vet.

I'd much rather run up a client's vet bill unnecessarily than risk her pet's health.

Do You Need an Infirmary?

A related question is whether to maintain isolation runs for sick animals. My thoughts are that the vets already have such facilities, and that the last thing my other boarders need is exposure to contagious diseases. Ergo, I don't maintain an infirmary.

Special Privileges for Friendly Dogs

When engaged in what I call "puttering around" in the kennels, I often let a dog out to toddle about inside the building. I don't do this when working with powerful cleaners and the like—that could put her at risk. Nor will I let a dog out whom I sense would go from run to run, seeing what kind of trouble she could stir up. But with friendly dogs whom I have come to know, ones who appreciate the chance for human contact and exercise, why not? It gives them a break from boredom and makes them feel special, and I enjoy the company.

What about bringing a boarder into your home for a time? My answer is another question: "Why not?" Many of the dogs you board are housepets, and allowing those whom you feel are trustworthy to visit you *en casa* is a bonus for your clients and for their pets—and for you.

Coping with the Death of a Boarder

Someday, a dog will die at your kennels. That harsh statement reflects a reality of the business. I've been fortunate to have it happen only once.

When I board an old dog, or one with a history of serious medical problems, I visit with the owner. "Look, we both know Fritzie's getting on in years (or hasn't been well). I have to know your preference should her time come while she's with me." My question, of course, is what the owner would like done with the body. Though some callous souls have said, "Take her to the landfill," most have requested that I take their pet to their vet, which is what I would do should any boarder pass away.

In such a sad circumstance, should you charge the owner a transporting fee? Of course not. Send a sympathy card.

Feeding
Kibble Storage

Mentioned in Chapter 5, "Equipment and Supplies," is the notion of storing dry food in large, labeled, metal or plastic trash cans. Such units are easily obtainable and inexpensive, and they preserve freshness by repelling pests and moisture. Some dogfood manufacturers provide storage containers if you use their products. Although getting containers free will not save you a lot of money, the idea is worth exploring.

Use lockable containers to prevent invasion by a dog who manages to escape from her run. True, runs are designed to be escape-proof, but canine magicians do exist. I've met some who possessed astounding breakout abilities. Also, you can forget to lock a run; while that should never happen, Murphy's Law and human fallibility make it possible.

Some major dogfood manufacturers recommend against storing their products in any container other than the packaging in which it is merchandised. Plastic containers, they claim, and the tin element present in metal ones, can draw out and otherwise damage nutrients from kibble that comes in contact with the container, greatly reducing the food's nutritional value. I have little formal knowledge about chemistry but sense that these claims may be valid, and in any case I see no reason to dispute the guidance. I still store the food in locking containers, for the

Be sure to place the entire food sack into the container.

reasons stated above, but I don't empty the food bags into the cans; I place entire sacks in the containers. At feeding times, after scooping out the amounts needed, I fold the surplus packaging over the food to close the sack. Kibble manufacturing representatives assure me that this method of storage ensures their products will retain their nutritional value, since the food never comes into contact with the container.

Mealtime

Though very young dogs may require a noon meal, feed other boarders twice daily: morning and evening. This is preferable to a single daily feeding for several reasons, the most important being that a massive ingestion of protein can trigger *torsion* (more commonly known as *bloat*), which can easily be fatal. The twice-daily feeding schedule also increases the number of pleasant events the boarders have to look forward to. Further, it facilitates run cleaning, since it tends to cause most dogs to eliminate within minutes of each other, rather than throughout the day since scheduled feedings tend to cause "scheduled" eliminations.

Feeding boarders twice daily also makes for a quieter kennel. Following occasional post-meal friskiness by younger animals, most dogs settle down and snooze after a meal. This tendency is especially noticeable after the evening meal, which should be presented around sundown. That's a time when dogs naturally eat. In any case, don't feed during a hot time of day. Doing so can cause dogs to regurgitate.

Although my own dogs and most of my boarders know to eat their food when it's there, some owners leave their pet's food bowl down throughout the day, a practice known as *free* feeding, and I observe owners' routines whenever possible. This is especially important with older boarders; why upset the routine of an old dog that is set and secure in her ways? Being separated from her people is stressful enough. Imposing your meal policy may guarantee that she won't eat during her stay.

Even with younger dogs, however, I don't leave food bowls in the runs after the evening feeding, regardless of the owner's feeding practices. This is because a dog who has access to food at all hours is likely to foul her run, and possibly her sleep blanket and herself, during the night, which can make for an ungodly mess by morning. It is also upsetting for other boarders to hear a neighbor enjoying a two-in-the-morning snack, and realizing that they have nothing for themselves.

A subtle yet significant aspect of feeding technique is to bring all the readied food bowls into the inside-run area of the kennel before giving anyone her food. This allows each dog to receive her meal within seconds of her neighbor, instead of having to wait while you trek to the storeroom, carry what bowls you can, feed a few dogs and repeat the process. The dogs can hear you preparing the food, and it can make them anxious to have to wait several minutes for their food to arrive when they can hear others eating. The practice of bringing all the bowls to the kennel room before handing out the first meal causes a minimal lapse between feeding the first dog and the last one. Also, although it's a minor point, I rotate my feeding sequence; in the morning I feed the dogs in the south runs first, and in the evening I feed the boarders in the north runs first, just to even out the waiting time.

Occasionally an owner may insist that her dog be fed only once daily. I accede to such instructions, but I realize that when this dog hears others chomping away, which is not the case when she's at home, she can feel left out. So unless the limited feeding is due to a medical condition, I see to it that the dog receives a biscuit or two during the mealtime when she would normally not be fed.

When two dogs occupy the same run, you may have to feed one of them outside and the other inside with the run-access door closed. Most owners who board more than one dog in the same run will tell you if

Don't do this unless you know the dog—put your face this close to the wrong animal and you may need stitches.

their dogs should be fed separately, but don't count on it. Also, dogs that peacefully eat side by side at home may react differently in a boarding situation. If you have any doubts, separate the animals for the brief time it takes them to eat.

Allow about ten minutes for each dog to consume her meal, but never remove a bowl while the animal is in mid-bite simply because an arbitrary number of minutes has elapsed. That would be unfair to a slow eater; moreover, you might be snapped at. But when ten minutes have passed, or when it is apparent that a dog has either finished eating or has lost interest in her meal, remove the bowl. Wash the emptied ones and cover those still containing food, refrigerating them if necessary.

This is also a good time to check everyone's water and refill those buckets that need attention. You'll be cleaning runs shortly, and after that you can turn your attention to other matters while the dogs settle for a time.

Dogfood Expense

There are two ways to accumulate money. First, earn it. Second, hang on to as much of that money you've earned as possible. A major operating expense is food. The question, then, is how to keep that cost low. There are two methods. One, use cheap food. Knowing that you get what you pay for, that method is unacceptable. Many of the so-called bargain brands are of such a low quality and nutritional level that a dog would be as well off eating road apples. I offer my boarders the same food my own dogs eat, which to my mind is the best kibble available. So, how to provide quality food at low cost?

First, buy in quantity. Speak with the manufacturer (not with the supplier; often their perspective is more short-term) and find out two things: the product's shelf life and its age when it is shipped to your supplier. Then determine how much food you can use during a time period that does not exceed its shelf life and how much you have room to store. Advise your supplier that you always want food from incoming shipments, not bags that have been sitting in a warehouse since the last delivery.

Second, make the best deal on price that you can. A useful lever can be your pledge to promote the product by telling clients that you use that brand—for both the kennel dogs and your own—and where you buy it. Offer to give clients take-home samples (at the supplier's expense, of course).

A Bedtime Snack

Every night, just before you shut down the kennels, give each boarder a dog biscuit, saying each dog's name as you present the treat to her. Yes, this raises your dogfood cost by a few bucks a week, but the rewards outweigh the additional minor expense.

Besides, you can keep the cost low by using store-brand generics. The nutritional worth of the snack is of no importance anyway. Nutrition is what dogfood is for. The value of a nightly biscuit is that each animal receives a little extra attention. For just a moment, pooch has contact with a human. She hears her name and receives a morsel. It's a pleasant moment for her, both in sensation and emotion. It is caring, and dogs know a lot about caring.

Take note: *hand* each dog her biscuit. You may not wish to open each run gate, but don't merely toss the tidbit into her run. You shouldn't be bitten as long as you keep your fingers outside the chainlink. If a dog lunges for the treat, yank the biscuit back, offer eye contact, stand still and remain silent. The dog will soon look at your eyes, to question them. Then calmly say, "Easy," and slowly present the goodie again. The word may be meaningless to her, but dogs are quick to understand your tone. Stretch the word out to aid communication: "Eeeeasy." After a few tries that leave the animal coming up empty, she'll get the idea and soften her approach.

Among other benefits, the presleep snack makes for a quiet kennel at night. The dogs soon learn that the snack precedes sleep. Regular boarders "teach" this to newcomers by example, and dogs are tremendous imitators, especially of attitudes. In that context, the biscuit has a mild sedating effect. (A friend who is a computer addict but who is not a dog person once commented, "I fail to see how food having no sleep-inducing chemical properties can affect an animal that way." I asked my friend if he had ever heard of Pavlov; he asked if that was a computer language and the discussion sort of fizzled.) As you may have surmised, it isn't so much the biscuit that causes the dogs to settle, it's the ritual and its effect on animals whose behaviors are extremely patterned by nature.

Cleaning and Disinfecting
Your Cleaning Routine

A good time to clean and disinfect all runs is soon after the dogs have finished their morning and evening feedings, especially the morning one. The runs, which may have been spotless prior to mealtime, will probably be loaded shortly thereafter. Of course, any run should be cleaned and disinfected between occupants, and any run should be cleaned and disinfected as the need occurs.

When cleaning outside runs, shut the run-access doors to keep the dogs in their inside units and vice-versa. Never allow a dog to traipse through disinfectants or cleaning solutions. To state that such chemicals can be hazardous to a dog's well-being is to grossly understate the danger: ingestion of some cleaning and disinfectant agents can easily be fatal. Of course, if all you're doing is a quick hosing of a run, there's no need to lock pooch away. She may enjoy watching what you're doing, and if she stands nearby, then you have an opportunity to check your coordination by hosing with one hand while petting with the other.

Cleaners and Disinfectants

Clean and disinfect runs with whatever compounds and products your veterinarian recommends. Not only are there geographical differences vis-à-vis the necessity to guard against certain diseases and parasites, but also for me to recommend specific brand names is to risk legal entanglements. Moreover, because germ resistance levels to cleaners and disinfectants can change, the best advice I can offer in good faith about what chemicals to use is, "Ask your vet."

An inverted bucket can provide an easy way to prevent leaves or snow from sealing outdoor drains, which can drive sewer gases into the building.

Controlling Flies and Other Bugs

In case no one ever told you that flies and other insects come with operating a boarding kennel, they do. The problem is how to deal with the cursed little buzzers. Chemical sprays are out of the question as they are potentially harmful to dogs. Electric fly-zapper lights are fine, but they are expensive to operate and they leave me wondering if they just attract insects from greater distances, insects that might not have visited the premises otherwise.

The best products I've found for controlling winged pests are the old-fashioned fly strips that a user unrolls and hangs from the ceiling. The bugs are attracted by the strip's sweet odor, but upon landing they discover the strip is so sticky that they can't depart. The drawback to fly strips is their unsightliness, especially when festooned with uncountable winged annoyances. Such a coating demonstrates how well the strips work, however, and I know of no danger they pose to boarders. Fly swatters are also effective, but anyone who runs a kennel is usually too busy to wield a swatter. It can also make for unsightly, splattered walls, and can frighten boarders whose owners discipline them with swatter-like objects.

Whenever you enter an outdoor run without first putting the boarder inside, lock yourself into that run to prevent escapes. Exception: If you are dealing with an aggressive dog, don't lock the door in case you need to effect a hurried exit.

The person who can't find time to spend a few minutes visiting with boarders is in the wrong business.

Special Duties During Winter

If you live in an area that gets snow during the winter, invert a bucket over each of your outside drains during a snowfall. This helps prevent snow from accumulating in a drain to the point of sealing it, which can force septic gases into your kennel building.

If you plan to top your outdoor runs with some type of wire mesh fencing, as recommended, and you live in the snowbelt, be prepared to clear snow from those tops, even during a raging blizzard. Wet, large-flake snowfall can rapidly seal the run tops, even those covered by widely spaced mesh, with a deep white blanket sufficiently heavy to bend the supporting side panels, including those made of chainlink. A quick and easy way of clearing overhead fencing is to enter an outdoor run (after first putting its occupant inside) and swat the underside of the mesh with the flat side of a broom. The snow falls through the fencing to the run's surface, you sweep out as much as you care to, and—while giving thanks that you had the foresight to wear a heavy, water-repellent, hooded coat—you go to the next run and repeat the process.

General Business
Talk to Your Boarders

Whenever you walk through or by your kennels, say each boarder's name at least once. It's a small matter, true, but only to you and me. To the dogs, it's an event, and a pleasant one at that.

Keys

Keep all kennel keys, including those to padlocks, on the same key ring. Use a short length of lightweight chain to attach the key ring to a wooden paddle or the like to lessen the chance of misplacing it. Whenever possible, key as many doors and padlocks alike as you can.

Plan Ahead

Periodically inspect your kennel from top to bottom, noting those matters that need repair or improvement. Then, during a slow period, you can have supplies and equipment on hand and be ready to correct the problems.

No Smoking Allowed

Don't allow smoking in your kennel. Clients may say that their pets are accustomed to it, but the point is that other boarders may not be. Dogs avoid tobacco smoke whenever possible (thereby demonstrating, at least in the case of dogs whose owners smoke, a better fix on reality than their "masters"). Dogs in your care should not be subjected to the harsh smell of tobacco and its harmful effects.

Similarly, if you yourself are a smoker, avoid the habit during arrivals and departures. Smoking may be offensive to certain clients. Further, it's just a good idea to keep your hands free when handling dogs. It's even a better idea to keep your hands free of harmful objects when handling dogs.

Pickup and Delivery

Is it a good idea to offer pickup and delivery service of boarders? Insurance for such trips will certainly be necessary. Other factors that may influence your decision are regional competitors' practices, time involved and the need for the service in your locale. I don't offer either service per se, although I have been known to pick up or deliver someone's pet under unusual circumstances.

Insurance

My best advice about insurance for any phase of your business is to remember that ours is a lawsuit-happy society; you should have a word with your attorney and your insurance agent. You might also look into policies offered through industry associations. I choose to avoid the insurance issue altogether, for two reasons: first, fairness toward you— I'm a dog trainer and kennel operator, not an insurance expert, and second, the fact that I have yet to comprehend any insurance policy's fine print. There are just too many *ifs*, *ands*, *buts*, *maybes* and *not-if-we-don't-have-tos* in the insurance game for an amateur player like myself to advise someone else how to proceed.

Should You Incorporate?

A related consideration is incorporating your business so that in the event of a lawsuit, you as an individual might be more protected. I can't tell you whether incorporation would be right for you; I only mention it as an option. If the idea has appeal, visit an attorney to discuss the advantages and disadvantages of incorporating your business.

Licenses

In your area, do boarding kennel operations have to be licensed? Are there business taxes you have to pay? Is a boarding kennel subject to the whims of regulatory agencies? As the answers to these and similar questions vary from region to region, I suggest that you explore these questions and related concerns with your attorney.

Kennel Helpers

Finding, screening and training kennel personnel is an art. Even before looking for a helper, though, acknowledge the fact that some folks, though mercifully rare, have no business being around dogs. They seem to exude a subliminal message that can bring out the worst in a canine, and they can knock down spirit just by being present.

Allowing for local work-age restrictions, often the best helpers are high school students. They often have enough maturity to handle responsibility but not enough age to be jaundiced in their views. Especially promising are youngsters who come looking for work instead of waiting for you to come find them. They often seem to have a sense of direction, a notion of where they want to go. They feel drawn to working with animals generally and with dogs specifically. That's why they aren't filling out applications at McDonald's or at a car wash.

Not only are high schoolers in an affordable age bracket, but also many are willing to learn that there's more to properly taking care of our best buddy than having a genuine love for the species (although that's essential). Their minds are open and receptive. They have yet to establish bad habits vis-à-vis *Canis familiaris*. Many young people I've interviewed are bored silly with school, understandably, and are seeking knowledge they see as being potentially useful, something beyond geometric principles and the trouble with split infinitives.

The good ones are loyal and reliable and aren't put off by hard work. Also, they can see your operation with fresh eyes and may come up with solutions for problems that your experience may prevent you from solving. That may seem to be a paradox, but have you ever tried for a long time to figure out how to do something and then had an outsider comment, "Well, here's what I would do," and discover that the idea was a good one? I have, and have seen in retrospect that my experience was what prevented me from seeing the obvious.

The question for us is how to spot the winners and cull those who are either out of their element or chasing myths. My manner of selection is far from scientific, but it seems to work well. All interviews are oral.

They involve no forms, and they take place in and around the kennels, not across a desk.

Gender, race and so forth are of no more concern than are parental social status or grade-point average. A shy manner is tolerable; a withdrawn one is not. Calmness of spirit is desirable, but a chatterbox isn't necessarily a washout. Head-in-the-ozone types need not apply. Formal apparel isn't necessary, but spiked hair dyed green and nose rings indicate more immaturity than I'm willing to overlook. Cleanliness, neatness, comfortable attire and a relaxed manner are what I want to see. Remember, your clients are likely to see these people as well, so consider the impression you want to make.

My first question to a prospective employee is, "Why do you want to work at a kennel?" The answer's content is valuable, of course, but its tone is more so. Allowing for nervousness (which may only mean that the person really wants the job and is feeling pressure from trying to say things "right"), I'm looking for a calm, collected and decisive manner of response. "I dunno" to any question fails the applicant.

Next I ask, "What would you do if a dog snapped at you?" The answer I'm listening for is, "Get away from the dog and tell you about it." What I don't want to hear is any variation on "Smack the critter in the chops!" Such an answer ends the interview.

My final query, other than obtaining some background material (age, address, next of kin, driver's license, parent's permission—which I get in writing—any history of trouble with the law), is, "If you came upon a vomiting dog, what would you do?" The right answer is, "Tell you right away." If that's the applicant's response I pose a follow-up question: "What if I'm not around?" "Call a vet" is the correct answer.

Throughout the interview, I'm cognizant of where the person's attention is: Is it totally on me or does it tend to drift to the dogs occasionally? Though I'm not adamant about the point, I prefer that it be drawn to the animals now and then. Respect for one's elders is admirable, but the individual who never breaks eye contact is worrisome; he or she is usually too intense for my liking. Intensity may be desirable in some fields, but relaxed is more useful in the dog business. Besides, I want to see curiosity and affection operating toward the animals.

Some people have objected to my selection process, opining that it is biased toward flunking those who lack initiative and common sense. It is; I agree. It's intended to be that way. One parent called and asked why I expected someone to know something that had not been taught (such as what to do about a vomiting dog). This put me in mind of a few lines from Dietmar Schellenberg's *Top Working Dogs:*

A dog will readily, and happily, comply with any reasonable request. He usually knows already how to do it.†

My experience is that the principle contained in the line "He usually knows already how to do it" applies to dog people as well as dogs—to the good ones, anyway. They are empathetic and intuitive, not impassive or mechanical. When interviewing kennel help and apprentice trainers, good ones are not only what I seek; they are the only ones I accept. This is not so much a moral decision as one of efficiency: If there is scant potential, why bother?

Competitors

Many boarding kennels are operated by sincere people whose primary concern is their guests' welfare. But there are always exceptions: Some establishments are little more than slipshod germ factories where the watchword is the almighty dollar. The only saving grace of such operations is that they make for meager competition.

If an ill-managed flea farm operates in your locale, clients may occasionally make comments along the lines of "My! Your kennel is certainly nicer than Fred and Ethel's on the other side of town." Irrespective of the fact that the person is probably trying to compliment your operation to a greater degree than the comment suggests (saying you have a nicer place than a pig sty isn't really saying much), the proper response is to thank your customer for the kind observation, without making any disparaging remarks about Fred and Ethel or their facility.

The time-honored notion of never knocking the competition is valid. Doing so casts you in a bad light. It sounds like you need to put others down to put yourself ahead; that the only way you can appear better is by slandering others, the bottom-line implication of which is that you aren't much to start with.

Many people take competition-bashing to be insulting; it's as though you're saying, "I'm telling you what to think about Fred and Ethel's Kennels because you aren't bright enough to figure it out yourself." Further, competition-knocking is a form of positive advertising for your competitors because it implies that you're worried about what they have to offer. A client might just get curious and go see what that is.

---

†Dietmar Schellenberg, *Top Working Dogs—A Training Manual* (Webster, N.Y.: D.C.B. Publishing, 1985), p. 3.

Besides, you can seldom be sure whom you're talking to, and things have a way of coming full circle. A person may be boarding with you because the place where she usually leaves pooch is full. If so, any disparaging remarks you make about your competition will likely find their way home. Putting down other kennel operators can send a message that you are all a bunch of greedy amateurs.

Always stand on your own merits, emphasizing what you can do, not what the other guy can't do. If your customers wish to say unflattering things about other kennels, that's their option, but remain noncommittal yourself.

Choosing a Veterinarian

Should you not be familiar with a local veterinarian, perhaps because you're new to the area, meet and get to know one before you need one. An after-hours emergency is no time to discover that the doctor whose name you hurriedly gleaned from the yellow pages has an unreasonable fixation on maintaining regular office hours.

In choosing a vet, take your own dog to the clinic for a cursory examination and observe whether the doctor is at ease with her. Of equal importance is whether pooch seems at ease with the DVM. Should either seem uncomfortable with the other, look elsewhere. While there, check out the general cleanliness of the office and the exam rooms. Note the attitude of the clinic staff. Should you detect tension, frayed nerves, short tempers or a decidedly lax, uninterested or distracted manner, be on your way.

Not incidentally, during any visits to a veterinarian's clinic, leave your dog's obedience training in the car. This is not to say that your pet shouldn't observe good manners in the office, but a trip to the vet's is not the time to require precision heeling, out-of-sight stays and the rest. Believe it or not, I once observed an owner telling his dog "Stay, stay, stay" while the good doctor pulled porcupine quills from the hapless animal's muzzle.

Prudence dictates that two vets are better than one; when your primary vet is unavailable you will need a reliable backup. As with your main veterinarian, you should meet and get to know this second person before a medical need arises.

After-Hours Medical Care

Once you have located and established a relationship with a reliable veterinarian, you need to forge an understanding: If you ever call after-hours it is because you are faced with an emergency and you expect immediate help, including a house call if necessary. Accordingly, you need to have the vet's home number, not that of an answering service. A vet who declines to provide you with that number is unacceptable for your purposes. A two-in-the-morning attack of torsion is no time to sweat out having been placed interminably on hold by an answering service whose motto is, "We could care less."

Of course, you should never call your vet unless you are faced with a problem you can't handle—and if the doctor entrusts his or her private number to you, never violate that confidence by giving it to anyone.

When your vet plans to be out of town, he or she should let you know so that you don't waste precious minutes trying to make contact in an emergency.

Sure, all this calls for some concessions on your DVM's part, but remember that it isn't a one-sided relationship. As professionals, each of you is in a position to do the other a lot of good. Though it's true that to recommend or suggest a veterinarian to your clientele is to split ethical hairs, there's no harm in telling anyone who your vet is, or that you are well pleased with his or her service.

Fire Drills

What would you do if fire hit your kennels? Do you have a mentally rehearsed plan that you know so well that you won't have to think during the real thing? Uncertainty born of fear can paralyze decision-making during a high-stress event, so it's wise to plan certain steps.

What do you do first: Try to get the dogs out or call 911? I'd get the animals out if at all possible and *then* call the emergency service number. A kennel can be rebuilt; a dog cannot. Where should you put the dogs? In a large, fenced yard well away from the building. What if they fight in the yard? Worry about that after calling the fire department. What if a dog panics and refuses to leave the perceived safety of the kennels? Grab and go. What if a dog resists by snapping at you? If you can handle the dog, grab, toss and go. And if a dog appears overcome by smoke? Get the ones who can walk out first, then rescue smoke victims.

Lest there be misunderstanding, I am not suggesting that you conduct fire drills per se. It would be foolhardy to release a group of dogs into a large yard merely for practice—you could easily wind up with a war on your hands. As suggested, a "*mentally* rehearsed" plan is the objective, so that if faced with a "seconds count" calamity you'd react without needing to make decisions.

Further, I am in no way suggesting that anyone risk his or her life to save someone's pet, or that a wastebasket fire that can quickly be doused (or thrown outside) be cause for emptying a kennel. The ideas presented apply to a severe fire that necessitates calling for help, but that hasn't spread so far you can't evacuate the building at negligible risk.

Vacation Time

Everyone needs to get out of Dodge now and then. But how does a boarding kennel operator take a vacation, especially if your operation isn't large enough to justify employing helpers? Since it's a 365-day, all-hours business, you can't just lock the place up and leave.

Or can you?

Many small-business owners find they have to do just that. Since you work with living creatures, you can't exactly hand the keys to a neighbor and ask that she look in on the place from time to time. The alternative to shutting down occasionally is to skip taking vacations, become wedded to (or jailed by) the business, and wind up working at a level of tiredness that does no one any good, your boarders included.

Of course, *when* and *for how long* you take some time off can make all the difference in your clients' perceptions. A month in the south of France during your busiest time of year is not a study in shrewd management, but a week or two during a traditionally slow period should cause few client relations problems.

Attitude

Image

Successful businesses seldom happen by accident. They outdo the competition by offering something the other guy can't or won't. In a locale having several kennels, what can you provide that your competitors can't? You have runs, they have runs. Your facilities are clean; perhaps theirs are as well. You're pleasant with people; they are cordial also. So why is one kennel booked up for weeks at a time while the others are just getting by? The answer is contained in this section's title: attitude.

I'm not just talking about attitude toward owners. That's part of it, sure, but it isn't the sum. As long as you treat people courteously, most will allow a "dog person" some idiosyncrasies. To a degree, they expect someone who makes a living with dogs to be somewhat odd. The point is that a kennel operator can be the most personable soul in the county, but if he or she exhibits no genuine caring toward the dogs, if the attitude toward the animals is impersonal, indulgent or plastic, the business won't flourish.

Think about it—put yourself in an owner's place. You have a dog, perhaps one you raised from a puppy. She isn't an ornament, she's family. You're about to embark on a vacation, and one of your last chores is to entrust your pal's well-being to a stranger. Would you rather hand your leash to a "professional business person" or an obviously "caring dog person"? Will you be offended if the kenneler greets the animal before shaking your hand? Will you feel affronted if her concern centers more on how your pet is responding to the new surroundings than in chatting with you? How would you feel if you were greeted by a perpetual smiler who pumped your hand until you wondered if you were going to get it back, who took your leash without much more than a glance at your pet, and who talked about your pet as though she weren't there? This person might pat pooch a time or two, but if you look closely you will see that the action is perfunctory, not heartfelt. That description doesn't fit anyone with whom I would leave my dog.

Incarceration or Caring Confinement?

A boarded dog finds she is restricted to a much smaller area than she's accustomed to. She finds herself trapped in a foreign place, her routine is altered, she's around strangers (canine and human) and her people aren't there. It's a stressful situation for her, especially if it's her first time being boarded. The question, though, is whether the animal is in a run or a cell. The determinant lies in attitude—yours.

When owners board a pet, they're hiring your space, true, but they're also buying your time, knowledge, understanding, patience and caring. When a new dog arrives, spend a few moments with her. When you find a spilled water bucket, don't presume the animal was being mischievous. For all you know, it was an accident. When you board a dog to whom you are not particularly drawn, one who perhaps growls at you for no apparent reason, remember that the animal by her very nature is more likely to be reacting than acting, and that maybe part of the problem lies with you. Perhaps you are unconsciously sending a message that troubles the dog. No, you don't have to tolerate untoward hostility or bad-actor, destructive tendencies, but it's crucial to remember that no dog is with you for the express purpose of gaining your approval. Any kennel operator looks forward to the arrival of some animals and to the departure of others. That truth has as much to do with human nature as with canine predispositions and habits. At home, that dog is a part of the family, which is why the owner is willing to go to the time, trouble and expense of boarding her in the first place. Your end of the bargain is to always remember that regardless of how you feel about a certain animal, that dog is precious to someone, as your pets are to you.

Reflection

Ay, in the catalogue ye go for men;
As hounds and greyhounds, mongrels, spaniels, curs,
Sloughs, water-rugs and demi-wolves, are clept
All by the name of dogs: the valued file
Distinguishes the swift, the slow, the subtle,
The housekeeper, the hunter, every one
According to the gift which bounteous nature
Hath in him closed.

MACBETH, SHAKESPEARE, ACT III, SC I, L.93

Record Keeping

Bookkeeping: necessary evil? Valuable tool? Whatever your view, it's a fact of life for any business. I've examined intricate computerized systems capable of producing voluminous statistics. I've also seen bare-bones accounting with a cigar box for receipts and a notebook for scratching totals. The best system for you is one you are comfortable with that produces accurate information while causing the fewest headaches.

This chapter describes a middle-of-the-road, by-hand system for tracking income and outgo; it can easily be modified to suit specific needs. It provides simple tools for determining how your business is faring and establishes a paper trail should you ever need to substantiate your records.

Although I've provided my own versions of bookkeeping forms as examples in this chapter, office supply stores typically have basic forms like these that you can buy and use so that you don't have to create them from scratch yourself—by hand, by typewriter, or by computer. You probably also can buy "packages" that provide all the basic forms required for a small business for a lower cost than buying them separately. If you have a computer or are thinking about getting one for your kennel, there are plenty of easy-to-use computer applications for bookkeeping electronically.

Bookkeeping by Hand

To give you a framework for understanding the system I'll be describing, here's a graphical representation of it.

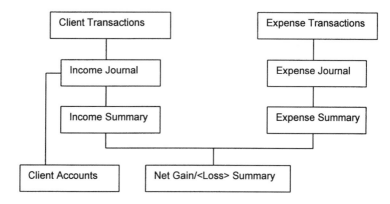

Basics

If you want to keep your bookkeeping to a minimum, here are the basic things you should do.

1. Open a checking account specifically for the kennel.
2. Deposit all kennel receipts and pay all kennel expenses through this checking account.
3. Record in an Income Journal all kennel receipts.
4. Obtain and keep receipts for all kennel expenses.
5. Record in an Expense Journal all kennel expenses.
6. Summarize selected data monthly from the Income Journal and the Expense Journal on Summary Sheets.
7. Total the Summary Sheets annually.

You can buy columnar paper, also known as accountants' pads, from any office supply store to use for the Income Journal, the Expense Journal and the Summary Sheets.

Income

A typical *Income Journal* would track the following information, each in its own column:

Column	Description
Date	When the income was received.
Receipt #	The number of the receipt given to the client, if your receipts are numbered.
Client	The client's name.
Days	How long the client's dog was with you.
Rate	Your daily fee for boarding the dog.
Board	"Days" multiplied by "Rate."
Train	Training fees.
Groom	Grooming fees.
Other	Miscellaneous charges.
Total	Total of the Board, Train, Groom and Other columns.
Tax	Total multiplied by the applicable sales tax rate. If services such as boarding aren't taxable in your area, omit this column.
Due	The amount the client owes. Again, if services aren't taxable in your area, omit this column since the Total column reflects the amount due.
Paid	The amount received from the client.
Charge	The unpaid amount charged to the client's account, presuming you offer charge accounts. If you don't, omit this column.
ROA	Received-on-Account payments from charge customers. If you don't offer charge accounts, omit this column.

If you do boarding only, the Board column reflects your revenue, so omit the columns labeled Train, Groom, Other and Total. If you provide other services, create column headings for those categories, and don't omit the Total column.

Record the appropriate information whenever a client collects his pet. Total the Board, Train, Groom, Other, Total, Tax, Due, Paid, Charge and ROA columns monthly. Verify that the totals for the Board, Train, Groom and Other columns equal that of the Total column. Similarly, the Total and Tax column totals together should equal the Due total, as should the combined totals for the Paid and Charge columns.

After you've ensured that these amounts are in balance, you should record them on an Income Summary Sheet like the example provided here.

Income Summary Sheet
Year _____

Month	Board	Train	Groom	Other	Total	Tax	Due	Paid	Charge	ROA
Jan										
Feb										
Mar										
Apr										
May										
Jun										
Jul										
Aug										
Sep										
Oct										
Nov										
Dec										
Total										

Each year, enter the total of each column on the line labeled Year, and verify the totals using the same proofs you used to total the Income Journal each month.

Expense

A typical *Expense Journal* would track the following information, each in its own column. The columns after the Amount indicate the category to which that expense is allocated.

Column	Description
Date	Transaction date.
Check #	Check number.
Payee/For	Who you wrote the check to, or what the check paid for, or both.
Amount	The check's amount.

Food	Cost of dogfood.
Ads	Advertising.
Equip	Kennel equipment purchased.
Travel	Cost of travel related to kennel business.
Repair	Costs of performing repairs and maintenance to the kennels.
Utils	Utility costs, such as electricity and water.
Ins	Insurance expenses.
Tax	Expenses of kennel taxes and licenses.
Other	Miscellaneous expenses that cannot be classified under the other headings.

Create additional headings if other categories apply to your operation. You will generally always need an Other column for both the Income Journal and the Expense Journal, simply to record oddball items that have a way of popping up.

Total the columns of the Expense Journal monthly. The sum of the totals of the columns for Food, Ads, Equip, Travel, Repair, Utils, Ins, Tax, and Other—as well as the totals for any classifications you may add—should equal the Amount total. Once they do, post the totals to an Expense Summary Sheet, as follows.

Expense Summary Sheet
Year _____

Month	Amt	Food	Ads	Equip	Travel	Repair	Utils	Ins	Tax	Other
Jan										
Feb										
Mar										
Apr										
May										
Jun										
Jul										
Aug										
Sep										
Oct										
Nov										
Dec										
Total										

Each year, enter the total for each column on the line labeled Year, and verify the amounts using the same proofs you used to total the Expense Journal each month.

Annual Net Gain/‹Loss›

At the end of each year, create one final Summary Sheet, as follows.

Annual Net Gain / <Loss> Summary Sheet
Year _____

Month	Total Income	Total Expense	Net Gain / <Loss>
Jan			
Feb			
Mar			
Apr			
May			
Jun			
Jul			
Aug			
Sep			
Oct			
Nov			
Dec			
Total			

Under Total Income enter the monthly amounts from the Total column of the Income Summary Sheets. Under Total Expense enter the amounts from the Amount column of the Expense Summary Sheet. Subtract Total Expense from Total Income for each month, and enter the results in the Net Gain/<Loss> column. The total of the Net Gain/<Loss> column must equal the sum of the year's Total Income minus Total Expense.

Record-Keeping Preferences

You can skip the use of Summary Sheets if you wish by merely totaling the journals annually to determine income and expense. However, should the columns not balance, a year of bookkeeping has to be audited to locate errors. Posting totals monthly to a Summary Sheet calls for extra steps, but can greatly simplify year-end work.

Another refinement is to omit the columns labeled Board, Train, Groom and Other from the Income Journal and the Income Summary Sheet. Merely enter all sales into the Total column. Categorizing of sales is internal information that may be of no interest to the IRS. (There are some exceptions to this; check with a tax professional.) However, since expenses must be itemized by category, don't eliminate the expense breakdowns (Food, Adv, and so on) from the Expense Journal or the Expense Summary Sheet.

One Final Record

If you allow clients to keep charge accounts, maintain a ledger containing an account sheet for each individual. A sample account sheet follows.

Customer Account Record

Client: _____   Phone: _____

Address: _____

City: _____ State: _____ Zip: _____

Email: _____

Date	Detail	Charge	Credit	Balance

Column	Description
Date	The date of each charge and each payment.
Detail	The dog's name and the dates of service.
Charges	The amount of each transaction from the Income Journal's Charge column.
Credits	Payments from the Income Journal's ROA column.
Balance	The previous balance (if any) plus total Charges minus total Credits.

The total of all account balances must equal the previous amount plus subsequent Income Journal total charges minus its total ROAs.

Other Useful Data to Track

Internal records and reports reflect information that you may not legally be required to keep but that can be useful for effective management of your business. Though such reports are limited only by need and imagination, consider the following analysis.

Summary Statistics

Date	#Runs /Day	#Runs /Month	#Runs /Year	Avail	%Occ	Dogs/ Day	Dogs/ Month	Dogs/ Year	Dogs/ Run	TD

Column	Description
Date	The day's date.
#Runs/Day	Number of runs occupied on that date.
#Runs/Month	Number of runs occupied so far for the current month.
#Runs/Year	Number of runs occupied so far for the current year.
Avail	Number of runs available for occupancy so far for the current year. (This means the total number of existing runs times the number of days to date in the current year.)
%Occ	The Year total expressed as a percentage of the Avail total.
Dogs/Day	Number of dogs boarded on that date.
Dogs/Month	Number of dogs boarded so far this month.
Dogs/Year	Number of dogs boarded so far this year.

| Dogs/Run | Number of dogs boarded this current year divided by the number of runs occupied for the same period. This will allow you to determine the average number of dogs occupying each rented run. |
| TD | Number of customers you have had to turn down because all your runs were booked when they called to make a reservation. |

Such a report reflects how your business is doing at any given time, provides comparisons between different time periods, and determines seasonal trends. "Turned Down" figures can indicate whether you should consider expanding your operation. Create a summary sheet for recording this data on a monthly/annual basis by replacing the Date column with one reading Month or Year.

Utilities Expenses

There is but one foolproof way of accurately accounting for a kennel's utilities expenses: installing separate meters. As that can be quite expensive, however, an alternative method is to apportion utilities on a percentage basis. For example, if your home has X square feet and the kennel building has Y square feet, the result of Y divided by X-plus-Y times 100 yields the kennel's percentage of the total square feet. You can then apply this percentage to your utility bills to determine how much of the expense should be allocated to the kennel.

I offer one caution about using the percentage method, however: Consult a tax professional first. Tax law changes like the seasons, and by the time you read this book, the percentage method may be unacceptable. Further, the percentage method may not be realistic in terms of your facility. If your kennel has one one-hundred watt light bulb that is only used for a couple of hours nightly, many tax agencies might object to your claim that—based on the percentage of square feet—your kennel is using, say, twenty-five percent of your monthly electric bill.

Long-distance phone calls are another utility expense. Keep a log showing the date and purpose of each call and to whom it was made. When your telephone bill arrives, match expenses with logged calls.

Travel Expenses

Any type of traveling you do for your business should be recorded. It may help you on your income taxes!

Travel Log

Date	To	For	Start	End	Miles

Column	Description
Date	Date of the trip.
To	Where you went.
For	The trip's purpose.
Start	The vehicle's beginning odometer mileage.
End	The vehicle's ending odometer mileage.
Miles	The number of miles driven during the trip (End minus Start).

Chapter Omissions

This chapter has not directly addressed such specialized topics as tax law, depreciation schedules or mileage allowances. Regulations pertaining to these and similar issues change too frequently to be included in a general book on kennel operation. My best recommendation for advice about such matters is to do what I do when befuddled about such issues: Seek the help of a professional.

Reflection

Order and simplification are the first steps toward the mastery of a subject—the actual enemy is the unknown.

THOMAS MANN
THE MAGIC MOUNTAIN

Problems and Solutions

9

I could have included this material in Chapter 7, "Policies and Practices," but the topics presented there are broader than the following "What if?" scenarios. Because everything doesn't occur in a nice, neat and orderly fashion in the kennel business (nor in any other that I know of) and because no one can foresee every contingency, it's difficult, if not impossible, to formulate all-encompassing, infallible policies. This chapter attempts to bridge that gap by covering several oddball matters that have a way of popping up. It also examines things that go bump in the night, or day, or any time in between.

PROBLEM A caller asks if it is all right to bring a bed or blanket for pooch.

SOLUTION Say, "Sure," and be glad you're dealing with a thoughtful owner. If clients don't inquire about bringing a little bit of home for their pet, suggest it. If the dog has no such article, provide one for her. It's a small touch, but one that makes for a more comfortable, calmer boarder.

PROBLEM A dog, for whatever reason, tries to chew or rip her blanket or similar article.

SOLUTION Regardless of whether the owner brought the item or you provided it, remove it from the dog's run. Ingestion of cloth can be fatal.

PROBLEM The animal fouls the blanket or dog bed that the owner brought from home.

SOLUTION Clean it. Sure, the dog shouldn't have soiled her sleeping area, but that's not the point. Never send a dog or her bed home dirty, unless you want to lose a client. That's the point.

PROBLEM A boarder has taken on what is commonly called a "kennel smell."

SOLUTION Bathe her before the owner's return. Although one could argue that the condition is the dog's "fault"—she may not have the cleanest habits imaginable—that isn't the problem. The problem is that the dog smells, and an owner detecting the odor won't conclude that it's her pet's doing, but that you run a smelly kennel.

Unless the owner requested it, don't charge for bathing the animal. You may or may not be able to collect, but the odds are that you will alienate the client. She may feel you are nicking her because you don't run a clean kennel. Make a note to ask her the next time she arrives if she would like her dog bathed before going home. That way you have a chance of collecting for the minor grooming service should it be needed again.

PROBLEM A boarder who has been eating well suddenly goes off her feed for several meals. Is this cause for concern?

SOLUTION One of the first signs of canine illness is the tendency to quit eating. Though it isn't a definitive symptom, call the client's vet—or your own if the owner's DVM isn't available—and let the doctor advise you about what steps to take.

PROBLEM A boarder consistently spills her food dish, sending kibble scattering in all directions. She eats well enough, but only after upsetting her food bowl.

SOLUTION   Don't worry about it. The animal is with you for boarding, not training. She probably does the same thing at home, and as long as she's getting proper nourishment, her flip-the-dish habit is more her problem than yours.

PROBLEM   A caller advises that her dog is on medication for allergies and that the animal requires umpteen pills and liquids throughout the day. She adds, "She's not real good about taking her medicine sometimes, heh heh heh."

SOLUTION   Ask the owner to define "not real good." If the answer is "She might nip at you once in a while," mentally translate that into "The dog will bite at me every time," and turn down the business. If the owner says the creature "is just stubborn, turns her head away," and so on, then you have to decide whether you want to put up with the hassle of medicating a recalcitrant dog several times daily. Also, be aware that a dog who is stubborn with her owner may be aggressive toward you, a stranger.

If you decide to board the dog, ask the owner to have her veterinarian call you. You want to be sure that the allergy is not some other problem, like a contagious disease. Then call your own vet and verify the facts as they have been explained to you by the owner's DVM. If either veterinarian communicates negative feelings about the dog's condition, realize that your first concern is for the boarders already in your care and turn down the business.

PROBLEM   An owner arrives to collect pooch and says, "I forgot my checkbook at home. Can I mail you a check?"

SOLUTION   If the individual is an established client, sure. This kind of thing can happen to anyone, as can finding oneself out of checks.

If the person is a new customer but the account is small, I'd take a chance on the person's honesty. If you refuse to wait for a small amount, you risk getting the cash but losing the client. The client may think, "They wouldn't trust me for a lousy ten bucks, for crying out loud!"

If the owner is a first-time client whose account is sizeable, go with what your gut tells you. Oftentimes, that's what running a business is all about. Yes, the person may be trying to get to you, or she may prove to be a valued customer. A large tab seems risky when you are being asked to take an IOU, but at the same time the account's size suggests the individual is willing to spend considerable sums with you. Keep in mind always, though, that if things don't seem on the up and up to you or if you have a bad feeling about the situation, in most states you are within your rights to keep the dog until you've been paid.

PROBLEM A client's check bounces.

SOLUTION If the check was returned marked "NSF" ("Non-Sufficient Funds"), contact the client and discuss the situation. Perhaps there was a mix-up while she was on vacation. If the check was returned stamped "Account Closed," insist that the client bring you the cash forthwith, or offer to drive to her home to make the collection. This person may be about to move, which could leave you holding the bag.

As a corollary, become familiar with credit practices and legal recourses in your area. Know your rights in the cases of bad checks or nonpayment.

PROBLEM An owner arrives to get her pet and advises you that she is unable to pay.

SOLUTION Keep the dog until you get the cash. Don't take a check from this person. Of course, if the client has a good history with you, you may wish to show more trust than I'm recommending. My experience, though, is that reliable people who are temporarily short of funds tend to make arrangements for payment when they call to make a reservation or when they arrive with their pet, not when they come to take the animal home.

PROBLEM A client who was scheduled to be back two days hence arrives this afternoon to collect her pet and tells you that she came by in the morning to get pooch, but you were not there. It is true that you were away this morning. Since your checkout hour is 1 PM, do you charge the customer for today?

SOLUTION No. Even if the individual were to arrive that evening to get her pet, don't charge for today. Be glad she isn't upset that you weren't around when she came by earlier. Apologize that your absence caused an additional trip and thank her for the business.

PROBLEM   In October a client makes a reservation for March. In January you raise your rates. You forgot to tell the client about the increase. What rate do you charge your client?

SOLUTION   The old one. Put yourself in the client's place—you arrive to pick up your pet and find that the anticipated bill of *X* is *X-plus*. Would you be pleased? Don't tell the client that you're giving her a break, either, because you aren't. You're correcting an error: yours. Tell the client about the new rate the next time she makes a reservation.

When I've increased rates I've made my computer print out a list of clients. As they call to make reservations, I advise them of the new rate and make a checkmark by their name.

PROBLEM   After a client has departed with her pet, you discover an error in the bill.

SOLUTION   If you undercharged the client by a small amount, such as one day's boarding, forget it. Don't pester the customer. Mutter to yourself something like, "You'd think by now I'd know that two plus two doesn't equal three" and forget it. It's a small thing. If the amount is significant, contact the individual and explain the problem. Most people will understand. If you overcharged the client by any amount, small or large, contact her right away and offer to send a check or, if she would prefer, to credit her account against the next visit.

PROBLEM   After a client takes her pet home, you discover that you forgot to return an item of equipment (food dish, blanket, toy, etc.).

SOLUTION   Call the customer, apologize, and offer to bring the forgotten item to her home.

PROBLEM   A client, while getting ready to take her pet home, tells you to keep the remaining amount of food she furnished for the visit. She doesn't want to be bothered taking it home and suggests that you give it to the other dogs; "They'll like it!" It is an acceptable brand, but one you wouldn't feed to your own dogs (or to boarders).

SOLUTION   This is less a problem than an opportunity. You could just thank the customer and throw out the food after she departs, but give it to your local animal shelter instead. "They'll like it!"

PROBLEM   A client told you three weeks ago that she would be back sometime this afternoon to pick up her pooch. It's 4:30 on Saturday and the store from which you ordered your eagerly awaited whatsis has called to say it arrived closes for the weekend at 5:00. What do you do?

SOLUTION   Stay put. Your clients and their pets come first. Settle for looking forward to getting your whatsis on Monday.

Let's make it trickier: Suppose the client is one whose arrival time is impossible to predict; she seldom sticks to her planned schedule. Now what's the answer?

It's still "Stay put," for the reasons given.

PROBLEM   You've locked up the kennel, the morning's labors are done and you're about to leave for lunch in town with a friend. Just as you're walking out the door a client calls, asking if he can bring Poopsie out within the hour.

SOLUTION   First, you must accept the reservation (presuming you have an unoccupied run). If it isn't convenient for the person to bring the dog to you later in the day, you might ask whether you can pick up the animal on your way back to the kennel. If that isn't suitable for your client, you have two options: call your friend and see if you can move your lunch date back an hour, or postpone the engagement until another time. Sure, it would have been nice for the client to have given you more notice, but like a hotel, when a caller wants to do business you have to be ready to accept it.

PROBLEM   You have a full kennel, and a client of long-standing calls to tell you that she forgot to make a reservation (or says, "I thought my better half had made a reservation"). She asks, "Can you help me out?"

SOLUTION   You can't afford not to. Experience teaches that there is almost always room for one more. Somehow, someway, find room for that dog.

A similar situation can occur when an owner arrives claiming that she made a reservation weeks ago—but you have no record of it. The solution is the same: Find a way to board the dog. You may have forgotten to record the reservation.

PROBLEM   A client phoning at 3:00 AM has a family emergency and asks, "Can you take Old Buster?"

SOLUTION   Find a way to board that dog. Even if you have a full kennel, tell the caller that you'll turn a light on and will be waiting. People don't call in such a circumstance unless their backs are up against it, and you can't afford to turn them down.

PROBLEM   What do you do if a client doesn't return? It's a fluke, but it can happen. Though accidents and fatal illness would seem to be the most likely causes, I have never known either to occur. What I have experienced is owners who left pooch with me and were never heard from again. They had planned not to come back. Either they couldn't find a home for their pet or they couldn't be bothered to look for one. Rather than take the animal to the shelter, they dropped him off with good old me. The question, of course, is "Now what?"

SOLUTION   First, wait at least a week, preferably two, before taking any action. Be sure the owners aren't likely to return, that they weren't merely delayed and didn't think to call you. Second, recognize that it isn't the dog's fault. She just lost her family (though it may not have been much of a loss), and she doesn't need further rejection, so be careful not to communicate negative vibrations to her. Third, send the owners a registered letter, return receipt requested, to their last known address. Inform them that if they do not claim their pet within a certain number of days, the animal will be put to sleep and you will sue them for the cost of boarding and for the cost of euthanasia. (Check with an attorney on this one, as regulations vary from state to state as to how long you must wait before assuming ownership of an abandoned dog.) Then, after the stipulated time has passed, get to work finding the animal a good home. No, we are not going to put her down—that's simply not an option. You put the threat in the letter only to shake up the clowns who abandoned their pet, assuming they receive your message. Once you find a home for the dog, you may be able to recover some of the boarding fees from the new owners. If you can't, though, let the dog go with the realization that her new people may someday board her with you. Yes, you will lose a few dollars, but bad debts are part of running any business. Accept the loss, realize that you did good by finding a dog a home, and get on with your day.

PROBLEM You need to run next door to a neighbor's home to drop off something they loaned you. Since you'll only be gone a few minutes, should you go through the rigmarole of padlocking all runs and locking the kennel building and the perimeter-fence gates?

SOLUTION Yes. Some chances you never take—this is one. Sure, the neighbor lives close by and you'll make your trip a quick one, but consider: Dog thieves see places like yours as gold mines, and they are very quick themselves.

PROBLEM You have to leave your property for a few minutes. Do you put all the dogs inside, or do you leave their run-access doors open so they can enjoy the bright, sunny day if they wish?

SOLUTION Put the dogs inside. Protection of the animals comes before concerns for exercise or sunbathing. Granted, the odds are that everything would be fine, but as I said about dog thieves . . .

PROBLEM You have to be away from the kennel for a few hours to pick up supplies. Is there any reason to padlock the gates of the unoccupied runs as well as those of the occupied ones?

SOLUTION Yes. If someone with devious intent were to crawl over your fence, padlocked runs would make it harder to get at a run-access door to break into the building. Also, a thief might correctly interpret an unlocked run as being empty. Make it appear that all runs are occupied, and let an intruder sweat out which run-access door might have a bad-tempered, large, unfriendly dog salivating behind it.

PROBLEM You have to leave the kennel for a time and are aware that clients may arrive during your absence. Do you leave a note on your gate stating when you will return?

SOLUTION Though that may seem courteous, security comes first. The note would advertise that the kennel is unguarded, as well as how long someone with evil intent has to cause harm.

PROBLEM Let's make it trickier. You have to leave the kennels for a medical emergency and you know that clients are on the way.

SOLUTION If time permits, ask a neighbor to keep an eye out for your clients and to tell them what's going on. Medical emergencies have to come before courtesy, of course, and in the interests of security I would still hesitate to leave a note on the gate.

PROBLEM A prospective client visiting your kennel comments, "My! What a beautiful Lhasa Apso you have in that run there. Can I step into the run and pet the adorable little dog?"

SOLUTION Though you don't have to share the sentiment's qualifier with the visitor, the answer to some questions is not just "No" but "Hell, no!" This is one such question. No one—and I mean no one—except you, your helpers or a veterinarian should ever be allowed contact with any boarder. Others may look but they may not touch.

If you're wondering, "What if the person who wants to pet the dog is a long-time client, not a stranger?", the answer remains the same: "No." Sure, everything is probably on the up and up, but consider: What if the dog were to bite the person? Or what if the individual fell and suffered an injury while in the run? In either case, you could find yourself on the receiving end of a lawsuit. It also shows the client just how protective you are of their dog when under your care.

PROBLEM A stranger appears at your gate. She tells you that yours is a beautiful kennel and asks to look around. You notice that the person's vehicle is carrying out-of-state (or out-of-county) license plates. Well?

SOLUTION Deflect the request by saying you just don't have time just then, but perhaps they could come back later. Ask a few questions along the theme of "Do you live around here?" If the answer is no, then ferret out why the person wants to visit your kennel. There are hundreds of legitimate reasons why someone from another area might want to look your kennel over. Perhaps the individual is thinking of building one herself, was sincere in her opening compliment, and is looking for some pointers. But those are some pretty precious dogs in your care, and it's safer to err on the side of caution in all dealings with unknowns.

> *Reality Check: By now you may be wondering, "Is he making up these scenarios or do they reflect experience?" Answer: My imagination is good, but it isn't that good. Dog thieves are a*

reality and are often well-organized and quite skillful at what they do. I'm not suggesting that every stranger be treated as a possible crook. I'm saying that every stranger is by definition someone you don't know the first thing about, and that until you do know something about the individual, tread softly. It's better to be a little standoffish than to risk the security of someone's pet.

PROBLEM A dog injures himself while in your care, perhaps nicking a leg on chainlink while trying to escape (don't think it can't happen). Who pays the vet bill?

SOLUTION You do. Yes, it was the dog's "fault," but the animal was *in your care.* Handing an owner a bill for a few stitches and some antibiotics for an injury incurred at your facility almost guarantees that you won't see that person (or her friends) again. You may, however, become acquainted with her attorney.

PROBLEM A dog develops kennel cough a few days after going home. Who pays for her treatment?

SOLUTION You do, or at least you make the offer. Point out that no other boarders have developed the condition, but never leave an owner with the impression that her dog got sick at your kennel and you didn't even offer to do anything about it.

PROBLEM A dog becomes ill and you have less than total confidence in the client's veterinarian. Whom do you contact for treatment? The client's vet or yours?

SOLUTION Only call your veterinarian if you cannot locate the client's DVM. To take a dog to your vet without trying to reach the client's preferred veterinarian is not only out of line ethically, but also exposes you to legal repercussions should the animal become sicker or die. Besides, the client's vet already knows the dog and her history. To arbitrarily decide that your vet is more qualified to treat a dog he or she has never seen is to presume knowledge that most boarding kennel operators don't have.

Exception: emergencies. Then you get that dog to the nearest vet.

PROBLEM A dog seriously damages some chainlink. Who pays the repair bill?

SOLUTION Certainly not the owner. Your facilities are supposed to be strong enough that a dog can't damage them. That's what an owner would be likely to tell you if you tried to charge for repairs. We both know that some dogs can damage chainlink (or nearly any other material), but that's not the owner's problem, it's ours. You might want to make a mental note not to board the dog again, however.

PROBLEM A dog escapes from your facility.

SOLUTION Find her. Contact neighbors, friends, law-enforcement people and the National Guard if you can arrange it, but find that dog! No other answer is acceptable.

As a corollary, if you didn't see the animal run off, but merely came upon the empty run, it's possible the dog was stolen. You should advise law-enforcement personnel accordingly, to give them a fuller picture of the situation's potential.

PROBLEM A dog that is scheduled to be with you for several days or weeks refuses to eat.

SOLUTION For a dog in strange surroundings to ignore an initial meal—or even as many as four (at a rate of two feedings daily) is neither unusual nor cause for concern. If an animal shuns food beyond that point, however, special steps should be taken.

Offering a piece of kibble from your cupped (for safety) hand to a depressed animal will often get the ball rolling, as will putting a single bite on the floor of the indoor run if the dog is too nervous to eat from your hand. Contact operates in the first situation, curiosity in the second. Should either technique have the desired result, repeat it several times, then place the food bowl in front of pooch's nose, depart, and let nature take its course.

Briefly rubbing a few bits of kibble along the dog's back before presenting them to her can be an effective fast-breaker. The food absorbs the animal's scent, thereby marking it "safe." Another useful technique is flavoring the kibble with a solution of a tablespoon or so of hamburger heated in a cup of water, stirred to obscurity, and allowed to cool. Meat juice dripped over kibble can be equally effective. Should a dog refuse nourishment for more than two days, however, contact the client's veterinarian.

PROBLEM You discover that a boarder is a stool eater.

SOLUTION Keep the animal's run free of stools, thereby eliminating the problem. Sure, you clean the runs several times daily as it is, but keep an eye on this particular dog so you can tell when her run needs to be cleaned again. Make sure the owner knows of this animal's problem, not as a complaint or derogatory comment, but in the sense of telling a client something she may not know about her pet.

PROBLEM You board a dog who consistently eliminates in her indoor run, where she sleeps.

SOLUTION Keep the animal outside as much as possible, bathe her as needed and be grateful she isn't your pet.

PROBLEM A dog is a perpetual fence fighter, initiating a war with her neighbors at the drop of a hat.

SOLUTION Move the fighter to another run, preferably to one adjacent to an empty run. If that isn't possible, briefly turn a water hose on the animal the instant she fires, aiming for the body rather than the head, admonishing "No!" just as the water hits her. Drenching the dog is neither desirable nor necessary for this approach to be effective; the startle response and your disapproval are the keys. Keep in mind, I'm discussing a confirmed fence fighter here, one who might try to rip off another boarder's ear or be injured herself, not a fence player or a dog who occasionally and briefly tells her neighbor to take a hike. In any case, avoid the technique if winter is in full roar, and consider caging the offender.

PROBLEM A dog who seemed fine upon arrival becomes gradually more nervous until she seems frantic. She salivates to the point of foaming, regurgitates, and has attacks of bloody diarrhea.

SOLUTION Contact the client's veterinarian immediately. If the doctor is unavailable, contact your vet. In either case, let the DVM call the shots.

PROBLEM Soon after arrival, a dog begins to cry and generally carry on, even to the point of howling. You recognize from her aspect and timbre that she's not manifesting any sort of "bad actor" syndrome; she is lonely, and perhaps a bit frightened.

SOLUTION Spend a little time with her. Pet her and talk with her, but keep your visit welcoming and brief, not consoling or prolonged. Protracted reassurance will only perpetuate the problem. There are some things only the dogs themselves can sort out.

PROBLEM A client arrives to board a dog who appears ill. The customer assures you that the animal is just nervous, but your gut tells says the dog is sick. Now what?

SOLUTION Don't let that dog into your kennel, or even onto your grounds. Admittedly, this is a touchy situation: You have reserved space to board the dog, the owner is itching to leave for her vacation and you aren't a veterinarian but a voice in the back of your mind is telling you, "Look out!" Tell the client that you feel the animal is infirm and that you can't board a dog you sense is sick. Offer to let the owner use your phone to see about having her veterinarian examine the pooch, but unless a vet in whom you have faith tells you that the dog is healthy, protect your other boarders.

PROBLEM A client who made a reservation last month arrives to board her pet, but it's obvious the animal is in season. You have a policy of not accepting bitches in estrus. What do you do?

SOLUTION Reconcile yourself to the fact that you may lose this individual's business for all time when you tell her that you don't take females in heat. You can offer to call other kennels and local vets to try to find her a place, but putting a female in season around males can lead to a multiplicity of major problems. If you have a policy against boarding bitches in season, stick to it.

PROBLEM A client arrives to board his large, friendly but unruly dog, and as you take the leash the animal bounds away, nearly jerking you out of your socks. Let's say you're a trainer and you sense that one good leash pop will dissuade the dog from further foolishness.

SOLUTION Keep the knowledge to yourself. The animal is there for boarding, not training. Popping the dog's leash may convey that you won't endure such antics, but it may also cost you a customer. The client obviously knows nothing about training, and permitting the dog to discover that the leash is finite may appear cruel to the owner. Mention that pooch could profit from some obedience training, and if the individual is receptive, sign him up for your next class or—if you aren't a trainer—recommend one in whom you have confidence.

PROBLEM A caller wants to board a dog trained for personal protection. Do you accept the business?

SOLUTION This kind of inquiry can happen more often than you might think. My policy is to take the animal, but only if I did the training. I've met too many "professionally trained" guard dogs that had the psychological stability of flash paper.

PROBLEM This can be even trickier. Owners of a breed champion (or field champion, obedience trial champion, etc.) want to board their "pet" with you. Is this a problem?

SOLUTION It could be if anything happened to the animal while in your care. A court might rule that your usage of "pet" in describing the dog in your boarding contract didn't apply to this particular animal because you were told ahead of time of the dog's status. That's when you can discover that the value of some champions is greater than that of some third-world countries. I've boarded AKC champions and titled working dogs, but only if they were owned by people I trust.

PROBLEM "Good heavens! That dog is standing outside in the rain in her run there. I wonder if I should bring her in and close her run-access door?"

SOLUTION During an electrical storm or a freezing drizzle, yes—do just that. Otherwise, let the animal do as she prefers. Rainwater is not only cleansing, it's cooling. If a dog that could escape a rainstorm by stepping inside chooses to stand in it, let her. She is obviously doing what she wants to do, and other than getting a bit soggy, she's not hurting anything.

PROBLEM It's time to shut down the kennels for the night and a boarder, often a first-timer, refuses to come inside.

SOLUTION Try dropping a dog biscuit on the floor of her inside run and closing the run-access door behind her as she enters to investigate. Or open the inside-run gate, eliminating the illusion that afflicts some dogs: that the chainlink gate is so close that it bars entry. Step inside the run and call pooch. Or grab a leash and go get the animal. Gently.

PROBLEM A client wants to visit her pet during the several weeks the animal is scheduled to be with you (this can happen when an owner is moving, building a new house and living in temporary quarters, and so on).

SOLUTION Though I will not accede to this type of request with a dog I'm training, my attitude with boarders is, "Why not?" Take the dog out of the kennel area for such visits, so as not to upset the other animals. Note the dates and times of all visits on your boarding record.

PROBLEM Even after reading several books on the subject, you still feel undereducated about canine first aid and emergency procedures.

SOLUTION Veterinarians sometimes offer classes in emergency medical care. Should such a course be available in your area, enroll. If such classes aren't offered, meet with your vet and see if he or she would be willing to offer a class or to teach you privately.

PROBLEM A caller wanting to make a reservation advises you that his or her pet is just getting over parvo (or distemper, corona, kennel cough or whatever—any contagious disease), "but my vet says that it is all right for her to be around other dogs now."

SOLUTION Ask the individual to ask the veterinarian to call you and answer any and all of your questions. If the caller refuses, turn down the reservation. If the caller complies (most will), quiz the DVM when he or she calls; then contact your own vet. Relay the facts as you understand them and ask how risky the situation is. If there is any risk at all, don't accept the reservation.

An acquaintance once commented that she thought such a cautious attitude was too conservative, that I play it too close to the vest. Perhaps I do, but as I asked her, "Have you ever seen how fast parvo can spread? Do you know the disease's mortality rate?"

PROBLEM   You open up the kennel one fine morning and discover that the chubby little pooch that arrived yesterday is now a skinny little pooch and the proud mother of several puppies. The owner gave you no clue the animal had been bred.

SOLUTION   Except in exigent circumstances, call the owner's veterinarian (or yours, if the owner's vet is unavailable), apprise him or her of the situation, and arrange for the doctor to examine the dam and her offspring at your kennel as soon as possible. Don't take the dam and her pups to the vet's office—have the vet come to you. The risk of disease transmission (or injury) to the dam or her pups is just too great. The kennel call will run up the owner's vet bill, and if you're an experienced breeder you may feel that you can handle the situation without assistance, but the purpose of involving a vet is to cover yourself legally. In a courtroom, a lawyer can make it appear that a breeder of, say, Great Danes, is not qualified to deal with the whelping of and caring for Bichon Frise puppies or their mother.

By the way, though it may seem appropriate to confront the owner for not warning you, bear in mind that it could well be that she was unaware that the pooch was carrying a litter. Meaning no unkindness (or not too much, at least), some owners do well to remember their pet's name.

Also, don't charge the owner extra for your time. She'll have enough of a vet bill as it is.

PROBLEM   Someone wishes to board a pregnant female.

SOLUTION   I won't do it, even if she isn't scheduled to whelp for weeks and the owner is only going to be away for a few days. Simply put, there's just too much that can go wrong.

PROBLEM   You are asked to board a dog for the mandated rabies quarantine period after the animal bit someone.

SOLUTION   No way! My attitude is, "Let me get this straight—you want me to accept into my kennel a dog who may have rabies? You've got to be kidding!"

PROBLEM   Your phone rings. The caller hails from wherever and wants to board her pooch with you while she visits with local friends.

SOLUTION There's no easy, cut-and-dried answer to this one. Consider a few variables. First, you may have no way of verifying that the animal is currently vaccinated against parvo, distemper, rabies, and so on. If the individual can produce a printed health certificate signed by a DVM, everything is probably okay (regarding vaccinations, at least). However, many travelers who take pooch along carry a vaccination record that they have maintained themselves. It may be that the notations appear on a form provided by a veterinary clinic, but without a vet's signature, such a record is worthless in terms of verification. Even a signed paper can lead you into the area of wondering if a veterinarian indeed signed the form.

Another point is that for all you know, the dog is currently recovering not just from an illness but a highly contagious one. Some canine maladies can spread like wildfire, and while the animal is *probably* healthy, are you comfortable taking that chance?

Consider, too, that, unlike boarding the out-of-towner, boarding any new *local* dog has a positive element to it: the opportunity to add a client to your following. In all likelihood, you will never see the out-of-town dog or her owner again (which you might keep in mind should she want to pay by check). That part of the equation makes me even less inclined to board an out-of-town dog. The best I can do is make a few bucks, but at what risk?

Of course, there's no need to hurt someone's feelings or to make an owner angry. Rather than tell the caller all the reasons why you don't take out-of-town dogs, merely advise her that your kennel is full. Lying is sometimes kinder.

Here are four tips for taking an out-of-towner: First, get the cash in advance. Second, *cash* is not a synonym for *check*. Third, house the animal as far from other boarders as possible. Lastly, treat the dog like any other; do not allow any residual misgivings to cause you to ostracize her from your attentions.

PROBLEM You have a remarkable case of flu, complete with fever, cramps, nausea, diarrhea, the lot—and you don't have a kennel helper.

SOLUTION Feel really sorry for yourself for about ten minutes, then go take care of your boarders. Today is not the day to perform a major cleaning or repaint the building, but you must complete the basics: feeding, fresh water, clean runs. If you're a trainer, skip today's workouts. A trainer who works dogs when tired or ill seldom accomplishes anything positive.

PROBLEM   A dog just bit you, drawing blood.

SOLUTION   Contact an MD and do as he or she tells you. If the wound is serious, respond as you would to any critical household accident: Get to a hospital emergency room or clinic, or call an ambulance.

PROBLEM   The following depicts a most unlikely occurrence, especially at a boarding kennel (which is why I've saved it until last), but prudence dictates that it be included. An armed individual, or one whose size is clearly more than you can safely handle, attempts to rob you.

SOLUTION   Let him or her succeed. Stay calm. Offer no resistance whatsoever. I'd even offer to carry the cash to their vehicle. Never fight for money. It can be replaced—you can't. If possible, occupy your mind by noting the creep's physical description and clothing. That'll be helpful to the police and may keep your fear at bay. Get the license number if you can do so safely, and note the robber's direction of departure. Once the perp leaves, call the cops. Then sit down, gives thanks that you weren't injured, and write down every detail you can recall about the incident, including what each of you said, and give a copy to the police.

What if the intruder threatens to harm or steal any of the dogs? It isn't my place to tell you what you should do. The smart thing, of course, is to realize that sometimes it's an irrational world, and that some situations are beyond your control. Personally, however—I speak here *only of myself*—anyone who would harm a helpless animal might signal that I'm next. In any case, while a felon can have my money, he'd have to go through me to get at a dog. Smart? No. Stupid? Probably. Inevitable? Bet on it.

Reflection

PROBLEM   After a day of dealing with two fence fighters, a feces eater who also urinates in his water bucket, a plugged-up septic line, two cancellations for what was supposed to be a booked-up weekend and a fear-biter whose lunge caused you to whack your head as you jumped away, an old dog who's been with you many times licks your hand as you set down her evening meal. Your eyes meet, her tail wags, and as you pet her soft fur she tiredly leans against you. The day sweetens beyond measure, and the chronic howler in the next run seems miles away.

SOLUTION   Enjoy the moment.

JOEL M. MCMAINS

Lessons from the Best Teacher

The closing chapter of each of my Howell Book House training and care books presents anecdotes, and I'd like to continue that tradition here. My intention is to provide some light reading containing not-so-light messages.

Guilty As Charged? Or Prejudged?

While I was puttering in the storeroom, the Labrador spilled her water bucket for the third time in as many hours. As I heard the bucket fall I thought aloud, "This is getting just a wee bit old." Cocoa had stayed with me several times before, and I had long since accepted that she had a mischievous streak. She was in no way wicked or bad-tempered, but more of an imp. Many times when I came upon her shredding a blanket, spilling food or knocking over a water bucket, her playful countenance said, "Gotcha again, didn't I!"

Anyway, this particular morning found me fighting a sinus headache pounding out the anvil chorus, and I confess that as I went to Cocoa's run, I harbored impure, less-than-professional thoughts. But when I arrived, something was different. Her tail was down and so was she, emotionally. I sensed nervousness, anxiety and a dab of fear. I then saw something else—the remains of a disassembled hornet near the overturned bucket.

I entered the Lab's run, brushed what was left of the dismantled bug into the clean-out trough, and examined Cocoa for signs that she had been stung, sighing in relief when I found none. I stayed with her for a while in case I had overlooked something; dogs can die from insect bites. As I petted her, I felt pleasure from two sources. First, Cocoa gradually returned to her happy, bounce-around-the-place self. Second, I'd just received a good object lesson to pass along in this book.

The spilled bucket was probably an accident related to self-defense. But even if there had been no other evidence, no gone-to-God bug, could it not have been that Cocoa toppled the bucket accidentally as she scared the intruder from her run? Any number of explanations were possible. Moral: Never discipline for something you didn't see happen. That could bruise the spirit as much as a wasp sting could bruise the hide.

"Whoops!"

The Rottweiler's name was Hummel. Mine was almost mud the day the two of us reached an understanding.

Normally, I won't board a dog I can't physically handle safely should I have to confront him. But the owner was a dear friend, so I made an exception. The oversized Rotty was dominant by nature and disinclined to listen to anyone other than the gentle lady who owned him, but I figured that I could get through the few days he'd be with me as long as we had no physical contact.

My mind was elsewhere (characteristically, some would allege), and as I walked by Hummel's outside run I jumped a foot when he growled at me. "Hush, now," I told him. With that he hit the chainlink, stood on his rear legs and barked in my face, saying—or at least I heard him say— "In your ear!" Whether a dog is with me for boarding or training, disrespect is one attitude I seldom tolerate. I yanked open the run door, leapt inside, grabbed two handfuls of Rotty under the jaw and began a speech with, "Now you by God see here!"

Then I remembered who I had hold of.

Fortunately, I brought it off. I stuck to my course and convinced the amazed animal that I don't take kindly to being yelled at. I offered a final piece of advice, shoved Hummel away, left the run and trembled a lot.

Starting that day, Hummel's attitude toward me underwent a gradual change, and eventually we became buddies. In retrospect, going beak to beak with him was perhaps not the brightest thing I've ever done, but in truth I'd do it again. Knowing Rottweilers generally and this animal specifically, acceptance of his "You're lucky this fence is between us" message would have reinforced his hostility, making subsequent dealings with him even more dangerous.

Am I saying that you yourself should physically confront the next high-powered woofer you board? Of course not. I usually follow the course of *deflection*, which is ignoring low-risk contention or peripherally undesirable behavior to prevent either from escalating.

What I am telling you is twofold: First, as a boarding kennel operator you always have to know the dog and yourself—his abilities and your limitations. Second, sometimes you have to be an actor. Someday you may have no choice but to confront a Hummel on the fight—he may make the decision for you—and the outcome may well depend on the attitude you project. Remember, a dog who doesn't expect confrontation may be taken aback when a person responds with forceful confidence. If you radiate uncertainty, the dog may sense it and feel he's already won. Doubt in your mind can remove doubt from his.

How Do They Know?

Alternate title: "How Many Times I've Seen It Happen." The following composite stars a female German Shepherd named Miranda.

One Tuesday afternoon around 4:00, she started acting antsy, trotting back and forth in her run, barking sporadically at nothing in particular. I commented to my kennel helper that Mike—Miranda's owner—would probably be picking up the dog soon.

"But Miranda's not supposed to leave for a couple of days yet. Did Mike call and say he'd be along this afternoon?"

"Nope. Haven't heard a word from him, but I expect he'll be showing up within a couple of hours."

"What makes you think so?"

"Just look at how Miranda's acting," I said. "She senses he's coming."

"Joel, give me a break. So she's a little antsy. That doesn't mean anything."

"Maybe not but a pizza says Mike will be here before six."

"You're on!"

Mike arrived at a little after five and collected Miranda, my kennel helper dithered about and muttered to herself for a while, and I soon observed the truism that pizza tastes best when someone else pays for it.

How do they know? I have no earthly notion, but I know they often do. I've witnessed the phenomenon too many times to ignore it. An hour or so prior to an owner's unscheduled arrival, some dogs, usually those who are well-bonded to their people, become active. They sniff the air, bark, stare toward my driveway and communicate a sense of anticipation. Would I call the attribute spooky? No. Mysterious perhaps, but not eerie. It's simply another canine ability.

Messages?

Although the Beagle was female, her name was Barnaby, and in human terms she was over 100 years old. She was blind and deaf, and I remember her for her sweet nature, and because she was the only dog to die while in my care.

When I locked up the kennels that evening, she appeared no different than she had the night before. A little trouble breathing, but that wasn't new. Her head was shaking a bit, but that had been the case for months. I had no inkling that she'd be gone before morning. Fact is, I remember thinking that the next day I'd pick her up and carry her around a bit. She always seemed to like that, and to rest her muzzle against my neck.

At 2:30 in the morning, I had been out like a light for several hours when I found myself stepping into my slippers, grabbing my robe and stumbling toward the kennels before I was fully awake. Had anyone asked why, I wouldn't have had an answer. I just knew I had to get there.

By 4:00 AM Barnaby was gone. I sat in her run and held her in my lap and kept my hand close to her nose, so she'd catch its scent, so she'd know she wasn't alone.

Have I ever felt "summoned" to the kennels before or since? No. Did I perhaps hear a barker who quieted by the time I came awake? All the boarders were asleep when I arrived.

A non–dog-person friend commented, "The idea that dogs can send messages is ridiculous. You probably just noticed something unusual about Barnaby subconsciously, and it just took a few hours to sink in."

I smiled at my friend and nodded. "Yeah," I said. "That's probably it."

Look Out, Expert!

Although you may not be a breeder or a trainer, the public may perceive you as being knowledgeable in both areas. Occasionally, you may be asked to evaluate a dog. Although your first impulses may lean toward service, helpfulness and promoting your kennels, be careful. Be very, very careful.

The Doberman appeared friendly enough as he pulled his owner to my gate. The owner had called earlier, asking if I'd help him find a home for the dog. I receive many such calls, and since I often hear from people wanting a pet, I take names and phone numbers and post them with information on breed, gender, age and so forth on my bulletin board, in hopes of hearing of a match. Something in this caller's tone caught my attention, though, and while it isn't my usual practice, I asked that he bring his dog by for a once-over.

A few minutes of discussion with the owner found me on one knee in front of and slightly to the right of the Doberman. I was caressing the side of his neck with my left hand, and my right hand was near the left-center of his chest. The dog was enjoying the contact; all was well.

Suddenly the Dobie went rigid. His pupils expanded and he attacked me. I don't mean he nipped—he exploded. Full-mouth lunges and intense growling.

I learned long ago that the safest course when attacked is to move no more than is absolutely necessary. Remove what anatomy you must from harm's way, yes, but use as little movement as possible. It's akin to the notion of not running when near a swarm of bees: Swift motion can excite and attract them. My reflexes took over—I had no time for conscious thought—and I was spared injury.

To this day I can mentally replay the incident in slow motion with vivid detail and clarity. The Doberman's first assault was toward my face. I snapped my head back just enough that he lost interest and redirected his focus toward the faster motion of my left hand, which I was whipping up and away from the dog, knowing at a subliminal level that this would make it his next target, and that he wouldn't be able to reach it.

How close did things get? I felt the dog's breath on my face, his whiskers on my cheek. His muzzle fur grazed my palm as the leash stopped him.

At no time did I stand. That takes too long, and the animal would likely have reacted by taking me in the leg. How long did everything take? Maybe three seconds. Certainly no more than that. Did I see the attack coming? Yes, but only a blink before it began. Nothing in the dog's aspect had even hinted at hostility before then.

I tell you this tale to point out two dangers inherent in dealing with unknown dogs. The first is obvious: They can unjustly and without provocation launch an all-out war in a millisecond, going from dormancy to full-on and flat-out hostility in a heartbeat. The second risk is less obvious: Don't expect any help from the owner. Perhaps you noticed that I didn't tell you that the man "hurriedly pulled his dog back." That's because he didn't. My full attention was on the Doberman, you understand, but I was aware that the owner didn't move a muscle. He just stood there, his mouth hanging open, watching the show. Nor did he advise me ahead of time that the dog had—without cause—previously attacked several people in similar fashion, although it developed that he had done just that.

Yes, I should have asked if the dog was aggressive. I didn't. I forgot to.

Is this tale typical of my daily living? No, thank God. Such events are rare. So why tell you about such an isolated incident? Because you work with dogs, because you need to know what can happen, and because all it may take is one incident to maim you. Better for you to learn caution from these pages than from an emergency room visit. As mentioned, when dealing with dogs you don't know, "Be very, very careful."

"Look Out, Expert!" Part Two

No, this isn't the same story. It's the flip side of not counting on an owner for assistance.

Ying and Yang were Pekingese who were as alike—yet different—as their names suggest. "Ying's a lover," their owner told me, "but stay out of Yang's way." So, with my score in those days of "Ego 10, brain 0," I just had to test old Yang. Open the run door, squat, "C'mere, old Yang." Pat leg. Think, *I can handle any dog.*

Ever seen a "pro" run from a Pekingese? You would have that afternoon. The male Peke made Hummel the Rottweiler seem like a cultured diplomat. After treeing me on an indoor run top, Yang made a disgusted noise that sounded like "Smerf," and strode back into his run. I grabbed a broom, pushed his run gate shut, locked it and went and took an aspirin.

Message: When an owner (read: *amateur*) cautions you about his dog, listen up. Even if you're a "pro."

"Can You Believe It!"

This one didn't directly involve me. It pertains to a vet clinic/boarding kennel in another state. It's an object lesson in how not to run a boarding operation.

The owners of a large dog boarded at the facility asked a friend to pick up their pet so that he—the dog—would be home when their flight arrived later that evening. Mistake number one: The clinic released the dog to a stranger, relying only on the man's word. Mistake number two: The clinic had not kept the owner's leash; the friend had to use the dog's collar to lead him to his pickup. He drove pooch to the owner's ranch, and there, after opening the vehicle's door, couldn't prevent the dog from bolting.

Then the real tragedy occurred.

The dog spotted nearby horses and chased them along and into barbed-wire fencing. The horses' panic quickly spread to the man. Unable to catch the dog, he grabbed a rifle from his pickup and killed the animal. When the owners arrived hours later, mistake number three was discovered. That's right: The kennel had given the friend the wrong dog.

The owner's dog was still in a run at the clinic. He was of the same breed and gender as the now cooling carcass in the owner's corral, and because their friend had never seen their dog before, he had no way of realizing the error as it occurred.

Now, if this hasn't been enough to raise your blood pressure, perhaps the postscript will. The owners contacted the clinic and reclaimed their dog; the clinic called the owner of the deceased animal who, it happened, had never seen a horse in his life.

And the clinic's predominant reaction was to grouse about both owners' refusal to pay their bills.

As I said: how not to run a boarding facility.

Second Chorus, Same Verse

Although they had no experience in the business, two people whom I'll call Mr. and Mrs. Smith bought an established, successful boarding kennel. The seller advised them that they would do well not to change anything right away, but to make any changes they had in mind gradually.

As soon as the Smiths took over, they trashed the drop-off/pickup policy of 8:00 AM until 9:00 PM in favor of regular 9 to 5 hours. Within two weeks, they raised their rates over 20 percent. A month later, they changed the name of the kennel. In a year's time they sold the place, grumbling that they hadn't made a dime.

As I said: how not to run a boarding facility.

The Art of Compromise

Tiny was a male Rottweiler. I'm not saying that the three-year-old was exceptionally large, but his paws were the approximate size of Ohio. He was a bright, good-natured animal who spent a month with me learning companion obedience.

After Tiny's owner departed, I escorted the animal to his run. (In truth the dog dragged me to the sound of other dogs, but that's another story.) After removing his leash and collar, I spent a few minutes with him, getting to know him, and then I took my leave. As you know from

Chapter 6, "Daily Operations," I habitually put new arrivals in their outside runs, momentarily keeping the door to the inside run closed to allow them to learn that some things are for outdoors, not indoors. I followed this practice with Tiny, and after leaving him I leashed-up a Pomeranian who was also with me for training.

Tiny's run was visible from the training yard, and I glanced at him from time to time to see how he was getting along. He seemed intrigued with the metal sliding door leading to the indoor area, but otherwise he appeared to be adapting well to the new environment. Then, several minutes later, just as the Pom and I finished our training session and headed to the kennel, I saw Tiny near the end of his run farthest from the building, pawing the concrete while staring toward the run-access door. His head slightly down, his butt up, his concentration was absolute, and about the time I asked myself, "What in the world?" the answer dawned in "Oh, Lord!" fashion as the animal flew in full Rotty gallop-hop toward the door. He struck it with commendable force and I hurriedly told the Pom what fine work she had done, put her in her run and raced into the building.

It came as no surprise that Tiny was uninjured—he could have rammed a tank without hurting himself—but the door was finished. Dangling from its overhead chain, it was bowed inward as though kissed by a stick of dynamite. Of course, I reacted in my usual calm, unruffled, professional manner: "What the hell are you trying to do?!"

To this day I can still see Tiny's expression: confident, proud, a sense of accomplishment—"Trying? What do you mean, 'trying?' I've done it. When's lunch?" His abbreviated tail at full flutter, he was quite pleased with himself and I decided on a compromise: I wouldn't reattach the door if he wouldn't knock it off again.

Some problems are better deflected than confronted. Given the warm weather and the fact that Tiny probably wouldn't encounter such a door at home, I removed what remained of the thing and decided not to push the issue. In truth, the Rotty didn't know he had done anything "wrong." Heck, he seemed proud of his feat. I could have taken him to task over the incident, but that wouldn't have taught him anything positive. It would have just cast a negative pall over his new setting. Because he was an emotionally sensitive dog, as many Rottweilers are, I figured it was better to slough off the event rather than make it a focal point. As it turned out, Tiny showed no other destructive tendencies; he was as trainable as he was large, and I reattached a new door after he went home weeks later.

A "Cost" of Doing Business

Operating a boarding kennel can bring great enjoyment. As I once commented to a friend, "It's amazing that people are willing to pay me good money to do what I like doing—spending time with dogs." But, as with any endeavor, there's a darker side, a price, one might say. Consider . . .

Your phone rings. A client of long-standing is calling. You grin and think to yourself, "Great! Mugsy is coming to visit." You ask, "What can I do for you today, Fred?"

"That's why I'm calling. We had to put Mugsy to sleep last week. Just got too old. I knew you'd want to know, you and her always being such buddies and all."

So you spend some time talking with Fred, saying whatever you can to offer comfort. After a while you both say good-bye. You hang up the phone and hope it won't ring for a while.

Sure, Mugsy's passing is tougher on Fred and his family than it is on you. They raised her from a pup and she was part of their family for many years, while your contact with her was infrequent and minimal. Their house will be hushed for a time, yours will be back to normal in hours. But even though Mugsy's death doesn't even begin to upset you the way it does the owner, it does mist the eyes, and the day is less bright than it was. Moreover, and this is the price mentioned earlier, it won't happen to you once but many, many times. The owner struggles with one big impact. You endure many little ones.

Some People...

In Chapter 4, "Setting Up Your Business," I advise against too complicated or exacting a rate structure. Consider the outfit that had excellent facilities and good personnel but nearly sank itself under the weight of its own rate plan.

The day the kennel opened it had five different rates based on breed of dog. An impressive chart graced the office wall, grouping breeds under separate rate headings. All very neat and methodical. The kennel owner had but to look at the boarder, glance at the chart and assign a rate. Perhaps you've guessed the oversight. Sure, it wasn't long until someone showed up with a Heinz-57 and no one knew quite what to do.

So the kennel altered the policy to one of charging according to each dog's weight, which is fine for as far as the concept goes, but these people took it to extremes, weighing every dog they boarded like so much hamburger. Further, the kennel owner decreed that if a dog was even an ounce or so into the next category, they would charge accordingly. A kennel helper asked, "What about when we someday board a dog who's old and has gained a pound or two since we saw him last, but who's been a steady boarder with us since he was a pup?" I'm told the man didn't bat an eye as he reaffirmed, "We charge accordingly."

Finally things came full circle. One day a customer showed up with a large dog who was fractionally into the next category. The client pointed out that the weight of the dog's collar was enough to make the difference. The owner replied that the collar was part of the dog. The client said, "C'mon, Biscuit. Let's get out of this #*&@! joint and go someplace where they care about you as much as they do about fitting square pegs into square holes." That night the kennel owner called a friend of mine who was also in the business and asked for guidance: "What am I doing wrong?"

As my friend later told me, "He's a nice enough duck, Joel, but he's got no feel for people. Great facilities, good location, very well organized, likes dogs, but when it comes to getting along with his fellow man, zilch." Exactly what my friend advised the gentleman I do not know, but I can make a good guess. It was probably pretty similar to what you or I might suggest: a rate structure based on boarders' weights is fine, but plunking pooch onto a scale bespeaks too rigid an attitude. An experienced dog person should be able to eyeball a dog and determine his weight. And when the result is iffy, give the client a break.

Whenever possible, whether the subject is kennel design, quality of equipment, advertising or customer relations, take the long-term view. Those who don't can end up with memories of a short-term business.

When Push Comes to Shove

In Chapter 7, "Policies and Practices," I mentioned some approaches to try with your food supplier to lower the cost. A kenneler friend of mine found that his supplier turned a deaf ear to requests for a price break. My friend was on the verge of switching to another food, which he didn't want to do, when a light-bulb moment happened. He advised the supplier that he—the kennel operator—would not only tell his clients that he used another brand of food, but would also say he "wouldn't feed that slop (referring to the brand he was actually using) to a junkyard dog." The supplier relented.

I'm fortunate that my supplier is a longtime friend and that the need for such gamesmanship has never existed between us. However, I also recognize that one has to look after one's own interests first, and on that basis I have to admire my kennel-operator friend's *chutzpah*.

A One-Person Antibrutality League

Like the section entitled "Can You Believe It?", this one didn't happen to me. It occurred at a friend's kennels I was visiting, and I have her permission to relate it to you.

The Siberian Husky had been boarded at my friend's kennel for just over three weeks. When the dog's owner arrived to get his pet, I watched my friend nearly wind up with a battle on her hands—not with the dog, with the owner.

My friend asked the man to wait while she went to leash-up the dog. As she returned the owner hollered, "Cut him loose." So my friend dropped the leash and the excited Siberian scampered to the owner. Just as the dog neared him, the owner yelled "Sit, sit, sit, sit." I knew from being around the animal that he had no obedience training, but owners sometimes feel that their pets should be mind readers. The dog didn't sit, of course, but jumped happily on the owner. That was when the man struck the dog in the head with a fist and my friend lost her cool.

I won't detail her exact choice of words—they'd never get past my editor anyway—but her theme proclaimed that the owner had said to release an obviously excited dog, one who clearly didn't know from obedience but was overjoyed at seeing his owner—"But why I'll never know!"—and the owner's brutal response to getting what he asked for was totally out of line and would not be tolerated at her kennels. It was really something to see. The owner stood well over six feet and my friend was about five-foot-nothing. Even so, she backed the man up several steps as she laid down the law.

In the boarding business, like any other, one sometimes has to play certain games. Occasionally, you have to tacitly accept minor irritants to keep customers coming back. But when some dodo takes a hot-tempered action that could injure a dog, my friend sees her obligation much as I do: to protect the dog. If that leads the owner to go elsewhere in the future, so be it. Such occurrences are rare but they happen, and better that you should realize the fact now. It's part of the business.

Incidentally, the owner later took his dog through my obedience classes. Both learned a great deal about the other, and to my knowledge no repetition of the slug-the-dog incident ever occurred.

I Wish I'd Known

If you plan to erect a concrete-block kennel, be aware of an oddity about concrete-block fabrication: Although they appear uniform, not all blocks are identically sized. This is no problem when the length of a block is off, say, an eighth of an inch. A mason can compensate by adjusting the amount of mortar used to join the block to one next to it. The less obvious problem concerns blocks that are too deep. Since those exposed sides aren't mortared, the excess depth has to appear either inside or outside the building. That is, the choice is whether the outside or the inside of a wall will have an occasional slight protrusion.

Masons tend to place the excess of a too-deep block to the inside of the wall. They do this out of custom, knowing that carpenters can adjust the slight bulge with interior framing. But listen: Make sure that any such imperfections are placed to the *outside* of the building. Otherwise, if you elect to install vertically sliding run-access doors, you may find that some doors open stiffly and don't close at all. Why? Because if they slide over a protruding block in opening, gravity exerts insufficient attraction to free the door from the protrusion, so the door won't close. In that situation, one discovers the joys of removing the door unit, grinding down the too-deep block(s) to acceptable sizes, repainting the affected area—which necessitates keeping the dogs outside while the paint dries—and rehanging the door.

How do I know all this? Don't ask!

A Case of the Sads

Of the many dogs I've trained, Puppy remains in the top five in willingness. The male Labrador was with me for a month of companion obedience and was subsequently boarded with me often. It was during one of the boarding visits that trouble developed.

Part of the problem was timing. During one occasion when he was boarded with me for a week, Puppy's owner collected him and then—due to an emergency—had to bring him back less than 24 hours later. As I put Puppy in his run his spirit drooped; it was too much too soon. The fact that several dogs were here for training didn't help his morale; he came to see that they got leash time but he didn't. In the space of a few hours, Puppy became as depressed as any dog I'd seen.

Now, we know some dogs are manipulative: They manifest "the pitifulness of myself" for the attention it brings them. That doesn't make them bad dogs; it's often what they've been taught. But Puppy was as guileless a dog as you would ever meet. Subterfuge just wasn't in his nature.

So what to do? Various medications are available for bodily ills, but what of maladies of the spirit? Happy pills have been part of our national diet for years, and now they're being peddled for dogs, but I've never thought much of treating symptoms only. A boarding kennel acquaintance opined that it wasn't worth worrying about, that "There's enough to do without fretting over their state of mind." She was wrong, of course, since emotional well-being can directly affect physical health.

Besides, Puppy was special. He had gotten under my skin a long time ago. A part of the boarding kennel profession is the fact that you will be attracted more to some dogs than to others. Anyone who denies that has an emotional hide like a rhino or hasn't been in the business very long. Still, how to give Puppy that push to help him bring himself back up?

Answer: I added him to my training string. Sure, he already knew the work—quite well, in fact—but the few minutes a couple of times daily that I worked him lent purpose to this visit. He felt he was here for a reason. His owner had not found him displeasing shortly after picking him up—though I suspected such feelings were what was bothering the dog—he was here for leash time!

Training may not be among your interests, but should a dog you know to be outgoing and full of life arrive with an attitude lower than a snake's arch, just taking him for a brief on-leash walk can make a difference. Don't just cut him loose in an exercise yard; that won't do it. Spend some time with him, marveling at what a truly fine animal he is, petting him. Your efforts may be well rewarded.

Incidentally, I didn't charge Puppy's owner for the extra training time. The problem was mine, not the owner's, and no brush-up training time had been requested. Would I do the same thing—spend extra but unpaid time with a dog who needs it—even with a dog who isn't "special"? Sure. Wouldn't you?

The Need to Commune

Eor was a two-year-old wolf hybrid. He took well to being boarded and was easygoing and friendly, if somewhat independent, which is typical of such animals. He had a habit, though, that's worth pondering.

Every night as I'd begin to shut down the kennels he went outside. He stood in his run, laid his head back and bayed for a few minutes. Then he slowly entered his inside run, received his nightly dog biscuit and settled.

I've mentioned that mine is a quiet kennel, which is how I like it. But Eor wasn't trying to be a nuisance; he was merely going through his nighttime/sleeptime ritual. We could debate motivation all day long, but I sensed he was doing something he needed to do in order to rest, perhaps saying goodnight to that which guides him, much as a child might say his prayers.

Regardless of your rules and practices, always remember the nature of what you're boarding, and don't forbid a dog to be a dog.

That's It, for Now

The "Lessons" chapter is always my favorite to write because it takes me down memory lane, giving me a chuckle here and a shake of the head there. I hope you've enjoyed it and have gained from its content.

Reflection

The dogs eat of the crumbs which fall from their masters' table.

NEW TESTAMENT: MATTHEW 15:27

Postscript

An acquaintance once asked, "Why do you stay in this nutty business? The hours are long, the work is sometimes hard and demanding—there's certainly no real money in it." I grinned and shrugged, and said, "It's what I do, I guess," knowing the true answer to be beyond my friend's comprehension.

He'd never understand, for instance, the sense of joy and obligation I feel in writing this book. Here at my kennel I have the opportunity to affect the lives of many dogs positively. Through this book, I may reach countless more.

Most of my clients realize their dogs' specialness, that their pets are that extra sweater in winter, that cool breeze in July, the friend who remains when others can't be found. Some, though, have yet to perceive *Canis familiaris* for who she is. Through my passing comments and the conversations we sometimes share, however, perhaps their lives are enriched as they come to see their pets for the gifts they are.

I'm reminded of favorite words by Ranier Maria Rilke:

I love inseeing. Can you imagine with me how glorious it is to insee, for example, a dog as one passes by. Insee (I don't mean in-spect, which is only a kind of human gymnastic, by means of which one immediately comes out again on the other side of the dog, regarding it merely, so to speak, as a window upon the humanity lying behind it, not that), but to let oneself precisely in the dog's very center, the point from which it becomes a dog, the place in it where God, as it were, would have sat down for a long moment when the dog was finished, in order to watch it under the influence of its first embarrassments and inspirations and to know that it was good, that nothing was lacking, that it could not have been better made.

I agree that wealth may never result from canine contact—but richness does! How it surely does!

Canine First Aid

I do not claim to be a veterinarian. The following table is a compendium of several similar works and of my own experience. It is intended solely for emergency situations when your vet can't be reached, and it is offered with this caveat: If at all possible, contact a vet before treating any condition!

Symptoms and Treatments for Canine Injuries and Illnesses

Problem	Symptoms	Treatments
Anal glands	The scoots, excessive rectal licking, bloody abscess discharge	Have a vet clear glands; be watchful for ruptured abscess; check for tapeworms.
Animal bites	Skin tears, swelling, drainage	Clip hair around wounds, wash with soap and water, do not bandage, allow to drain; take to vet if deep or needs stitches.

continues

Symptoms and Treatments
for Canine Injuries and Illnesses (continued)

Problem	Symptoms	Treatments
Bleeding from cuts	*Artery:* Uneven flow, bright red blood *Vein:* Steady flow, dark red blood	*Artery:* Apply tourniquet between wound and heart. *Vein:* Apply tourniquet on side of wound away from heart. Use pressure bandage directly on cut; tourniquet not possible; release pressure at 15- to 20-minute intervals.
		Note: *Tourniquets are required only for life-threatening lacerations of large vessels (i.e., femoral or radial arteries). For most hemorrhage situations, using firm, direct pressure over the wound for 10 to 15 minutes is adequate to control bleeding. An improperly applied tourniquet can lead to severe tissue damage or even to the loss of a limb or a digit.*
Bleeding— internal	Weakness, gums pale gray or white, prostration	Keep dog quiet, use a stretcher to move and do so carefully; this condition is possible even when there is no apparent injury; take to vet immediately.
Broken bones, Dislocations	Inability to stand or to use legs; intense pain	Immobilize dog as best you can; use stretcher to move; use a temporary splint only on leg bones; don't try to set a bone—take dog to vet! Don't try to bandage or splint pelvis, withers (shoulders) or ribs.
Burns— all types	(specific burn types below)	With any burn case, take dog to vet if more than a small area is affected.
Burns—acid	Obvious	Apply moist solution of baking soda or similar alkali.
Burns—caustic	Obvious	Apply cold water; take dog to vet.
Burns— fire or heat	Obvious	If over a small area, apply a household burn remedy/painkiller.
Burns— hot water	Obvious	Douse liberally with cold water.
Diarrhea	Obvious	No food for 12 hours; if sure has not ingested a toxin, use Pepto-Bismol at 1cc. per 10 pounds of body weight; add cooked rice to food; take dog to vet if persists more than 12 hours.

Problem	Symptoms	Treatments
Drowning	Obvious	Hold dog up by rear legs to remove water; lay on side to apply artificial respiration; keep warm when revived.
Ears	Shaking, scratching excessively; inflamed ear canal; malodorous liquid	Clean outer area of ear with alcohol and cotton; take to vet. If ears are bloody or inflamed, don't use alcohol (it would be too painful); take to vet.
Eyes	Inflammation, cuts, scratches	Wash using eye lotion or boric-acid solution; use a triple-antibiotic ophthalmic ointment that does not contain cortisone as a general, all-purpose treatment; don't use plain water as it may irritate eyes.
Fishhooks	Usually in mouth, lip or foot	Cut off barb or eye-end of hook and work out very carefully; never pull the barb back through.
Fleas	Intense scratching and chewing	Have dog dipped at vet's; treat your premises; burn the dog's bedding; check skin weekly.
Ingested foreign objects	Coughing, choking, pawing at mouth; shaking of head often indicates object is in throat; persistent vomiting can mean it is in the intestinal tract	Examine mouth, tongue, gums, teeth; use handkerchief to hold tongue while examining throat; use fingers or tweezers to remove object; if it is deeply imbedded, take dog to vet.
Heatstroke	Lying prone, staring, difficulty breathing	Place in partly filled tub of cold water or douse liberally; must quickly reduce body temperature, especially that of the brain.
Hit by vehicle	Dragging, limping, cuts, paralysis, raw or burned skin areas, grease on fur	Keep dog warm and quiet; stop bleeding; support fractures with newspaper pads; be alert for shock symptoms (see below); protect yourself as dog may not recognize you and may attack out of fear and pain; carefully transport to vet immediately.

continues

Symptoms and Treatments
for Canine Injuries and Illnesses (continued)

Problem	Symptoms	Treatments
Poisoning	Retching, trembling, pain, convulsions, diarrhea, depression, weakness, staggering, dizziness, salivation, loss of appetite	Do not induce vomiting if caustic chemicals or petroleum products were ingested. In cases where it is proper to induce vomiting, doing so is effective only within 4 to 6 hours of ingestion of poison. Vomiting should be induced only if dog is conscious and alert.
	Note: It is a good idea to keep handy the ASPCA's National Animal Poison Control Center Phone Numbers: 1-888-4ANI-HELP with a credit card, $30 per case; 1-900-680-000 without a credit card, $20 first five minutes.	
Porcupine quills	Unmistakable; dog in pain	Hold dog between your legs or have another person hold him; then twist out quills using pliers, starting in chest area. May have to muzzle dog to protect self.
Running fits	Running about in wide circles; dog acts as if he is about to convulse	When dog falls, attach collar and leash; cover dog if possible; protect yourself, as dog may not recognize you and may try to bite; take to vet immediately.
Shock	Nervousness or prostration, weak pulse, shallow breathing, pale gums, glassy eyes	Keep dog quiet; discourage movement; keep warm; shock can accompany any injury or extreme fright; take to vet immediately.
Skunks	Eyes are often sprayed, causing dog to paw at them	Wash eyes well with boric acid solution; dry dog, then soak ASAP with Massengill douche or a commercial product; don't wash dog first as that makes oily scent-fluid travel over a larger area; examine dog for bites and take to vet if dog has been bitten, as skunks may be rabid.
Sprains	Limping, swelling	Cold packs for first 12 hours. Ask vet to recommend specific product for pain relief.

Problem	Symptoms	Treatments
Ticks	Noticeable by touch or sight on dog, often near the head	Remove with tweezers, taking care not to leave the tick's head imbedded in dog's skin. Once removed, burn tick and flush away charred remains.
	Note: If you are in an area with a lot of ticks, weekly (or more frequent) tick checks should be routine. It is not usually necessary to burn the bedding of a dog with ticks; they do not breed on the animal as fleas do. Also, a dog can harbor many ticks without feeling itchy.	
Vomiting	Obvious	Stop all food and water for 12 hours; then give small amounts of broth (cooled), cottage cheese, and bread crumbs; if condition lasts more than 12 hours, take to vet.
Worms	Weight loss, dull/dry coat, appetite change, depressions, diarrhea, vomiting, visible worms	Take fresh fecal sample to vet for wormers.

Index

Note: *Italicized* page references indicate illustrations.

A

Abandoned dog, what to do, 161
Acid burns, first aid for, 190
Advertisements, 87
Aggressive attitude in dog
dealing with, *134*
inducing, 32
Anal glands, first aid for, 189
Anecdotes, 173–86
Animal bites, first aid for, 189
Answering machine or service, 102–3
Attack from dog, 177

B

Bad check problem, 158
Bathing dog, 156
Bedtime snack, 131–32
Bill, error in, 159
Bitches in estrus, 167
Bite
animal, first aid for, 189
from dog, 172

Blanket
dog fouling, 155
owner bringing for dog, 155
Bleeding, first aid for, 190
Bloat, 128
Boarding contract, 112–15
examples of, *113*, *115*
Boarding kennel
considering offering services, 33, 40
designing and building, 45–81
bottom line for planning, 49
configuration, 50–51
construction and materials, 53–81
mapping out ideas, 52
equipment and supplies for, 91–106
nightly checklist, 105–6
Bottom line for planning, 49
Breed champions, boarding, 168
Breeders, considerations for, 19–33
paperwork, 23–24

puppies, handling, 24–33
responsible breeding, 22–23
whelping area, 20–23
Broken bones, first aid for, 190
Bugs, controlling, 133
Building permits, 45–46
Burns, first aid for, 190
Business
attitude, 142–44
incorporating, 136
setting up, 83–89
choosing a kennel name, 83–85
deciding how much to charge, 85–87
marketing your business, 87–89
Business cards, 88

C

Call-waiting, 103
Canis software program, 33
Cash-and-carry business, 118
Cats, facilities for, 81
Caustic burns, first aid for, 190
Ceiling, 58
Cellular phone, 103

Centralization, 50
Centron Software
    Technologies, Inc., 33
Chainlinks, 6–8, 66–67,
    72–74
    alternatives to, 7–8
    damage made by dog, 165
    mesh sizes, 67
    for run fencing, 12
Checkout
    problem, 158
    staying put for client's
        arrival, 160
    time, 117–18
Clarity, 83, 84
Cleaning and disinfecting,
    132–35
    controlling flies and other
        bugs, 133
    routine, 132
    supplies, 96, 132
Client issues, 121–25
    bad checks, 123–24
    chronic complainers,
        123–24
    dogs with unusual condi-
        tions or needs, 123
    giving each dog his due,
        122
    handling premature
        departures, 124–25
    intentional overbooking,
        122–23
    kennel inspections by
        clients, 125
    no-shows, 123–24
    respecting privacy of
        clients, 124
    socializing dogs, 122
    subletting avoiding,
        121–22
    troublesome, 123–24
Collar
    removing before dog
        enters run, 111
    removing for canine com-
        fort and safety, 30, 111
    storing, 111–12
Community events, partici-
    pating in, 88
Competitors, avoiding
    bashing of, 139–40

Compromise, art of,
    179–80
Concrete, 10–11, 53, 54, 58,
    67, 183–84
    problems with, 183–84
    for runs, 10–11
Construction and materials,
    53–81
    ceiling, 58
    chainlink mesh sizes, 67
    cooling, 59
    exercise yards, 74
    exterior doors, 55
    exterior lighting, 60, 61
    heating, 59
    indoor/outdoor run-
        access doors, 56
    in-floor radiant heating,
        59–60
    inside-run dividers, 63
    inside-run tops, 65
    interior doors, 55–56
    interior lighting, 60, 61
    labor, 77–79
    landscaping and decor,
        74–76
    outside-run dividers, 63,
        64, 65
    outside-run overhead
        fencing, 65–66
    perimeter fencing, 72–74
    refrigeration, 60
    roofing, 58
    run gates, 66
    run surfaces, 67–68
    sign, 76–77
    walls, 53–54
    waste disposal, 68–72
    windows, 54
Contact with boarding dog
    avoiding outsiders from,
        163
    communing with, 135
Contagious disease, refus-
    ing dog with, 169
Cooling, 59

D

Daily operations, 107–20
    arrivals, 109–17
    acclimating new
        boarder, 111

boarding record and
    boarding contract,
    112–15
    comforting dog, 116
    equipment storage,
        111–12
    housing assignments,
        110
    on-leash policy, 110
    quick general exam, 110
    departures, 117–20
        checkout time, 117–18
        receipts, 118–19
        saying goodbye to dog,
            120
        settling account, 118–19
    reservations, 107–9
Death of dog, 127, 181
Destructive dogs, housing
    for, 79–81
Diarrhea, first aid for, 190
Direct mail, 88–89
Dirt runs, 11–12
Dislocations, first aid for, 190
Dog(s). See also Puppy(ies)
    communing with, 135
    death of, 127, 181
    females in season, 125–26,
        167
    friendly, privileges for, 126
    high-stress situations,
        handling dogs in, 125
    mental state, influencing,
        114–16
    policies and practices,
        125–27
    who hurt people, 109
    with illness, handling, 110
Dogfood expense, 130–32
Doghouses, 13–15
    alternatives to, 15
    building from scratch,
        14–15
    prefabricated, 13–14
Doors, 14, 55–58
    doghouse, 14
    exterior, 55
    guillotine, 56–58
    indoor/outdoor run-
        access, 56–58
    interior, 55–56
Drowning, first aid for, 191

E

Ears, first aid for, 191
Eating
  boarder not, 156, 165
  stool eating, 166
Electric fences, 8
Eliminations
  constant, 166
  "scheduled," 128
Emergency(ies)
  equipment, 95
  fire drills, 141–42
  taking on boarder due to, 161
Equipment and supplies, 91–106
Escaped dog from facility, 165
Exercise yards, 74
Expansion, planning for, 49
Expense, record keeping of, 148–50
Exterior doors, 55
Exterior lighting, 60
Eyes, first aid for, 191

F

Feeding, 127–32
  bedtime snack, 131–32
  dogfood expense, 130–31
  kibble storage, 127–28
  mealtimes, 128–30
Feeding bowls, 91, 92
Females in season, 125–26, 167
Fence fighter, 166
Fencing, 4, 12, 65–66, 72–74
  materials, for run, 12
  outside-run overhead, 65–66
  perimeter, 72–74
Fighting dog, 166
Fire drills, 141
First aid, 169, 189–93
  learning to give, 169
First-aid kit, 16, 20
Fishhooks, first aid for, 191
Fleas, first aid for, 191
Flies, controlling, 133
Flooring, 58
Floor plan, 51

Food
  leftover from client, 159
  refrigerating, 60
  -related supplies, 91
Food bowl, 129, 130, 156–57
  boarder upsetting, 156–57
  removing, 130
Forgotten item, returning, 159
Forms and records, 35–38
"Free" feeding, 129
Frightened dog, 166–67

G

General business, 135–42
  competitors, 139–40
  fire drills, 141
  incorporating business, 136
  insurance, 136
  kennel helpers, 137
  licenses, 137
  pickup and delivery of boarders, 136
Good-bye
  kennel owner saying, 120
  owners saying, 114–16
Graduation from training, 38–39
Gravel runs, 11–12
Grooming dog before departure, 41
Grooming supplies, 96
Guard dogs, being wary of, 168
Guillotine doors, 56–58

H

Heat burns, first aid for, 190
Heating, 59
Heatstroke, first aid for, 191
Helpers in kennel, 137–39
High-stress situations, handling dogs in, 125
Hit by vehicle, first aid for, 191
Hot water burns, first aid for, 190

I

Identifiers and language for puppy, 32
Illness, dog with
  contact veterinarian, 164
  medications, 157
  refusing, 167
Image, 142–44
Incarceration versus caring confinement, 143–44
Income, record keeping of, 146–48
Incorporating business, 136
Indoor/outdoor run-access doors, 56–58
Infirmary, 126
In-floor radiant heating, 59–60
Ingestion of foreign objections, first aid for, 191
Injury to dog while boarding, 164
Inside-run dividers, 63
Inside-run tops, 65
Insulation of doghouse, 14–15
Insurance, 136
Intercoms, 104
Interior doors, 55–56
Interior lighting, 60, 61
Interviewing kennel helpers, 138–39

K

Kennel
  breeding versus boarding, 85
  choosing a name, 83–85
  clarity, 83, 84
  deciding how much to charge, 85–87
  basic price structure, 85–86
  discounts, 86
  fees for additional services, 86–87
  designing and building, 3–17
  doghouses and other living quarters, 13–15

Kennel *(cont.)*
    effect of kenneling, 16–17
    fencing and gate materials, 6–8
    first-aid kit, 16
    general care and comfort, 15–16
    location, 5
    record keeping of initial construction, 16
    run construction, 9–13
    security concerns, 8–9
    size, 4–5
    waste disposal management, 13
    helpers for, 137–39
    incarceration versus caring confinement, 143–44
    marketing your business, 87–89
    size of, 46–49
"Kennel smell," avoiding, 156
Keys, 135

L

Labor in constructing kennel, 77–79
Landscaping and decor, 74–76
Lawsuit, avoiding, 114
Lessons learned, 173–86
    attack from dog, handling, 177
    confrontations, 175–76
    discipline, 173–74
    messages, reading, 176
Licenses, 137
Lighting
    exterior, 60
    interior, 60, *61*
Location, planning, 52–53
Locking up kennel, 162

M

Maintenance tools, 97
Mapping out design ideas, 52
Marketing your business, 87–89
    advertisements, 87
    business cards, 88
    direct mail, 88–89

participating in community events, 88
    word of mouth, 88
Mass appeal, 83, 84
Maternity ward for breeders, 20
Medical care. *See also* Veterinarian
    after-hours, 140–41
    courses from veterinarian, 169
    leaving kennel to seek, 162–63
Medical supplies, checklist for, 93–94
Medication, dog on, 157
Motion sensors, 104

N–O

Name of kennel, choosing, 83
Non-climb wire fencing, 6, 73

Obedience class for puppies, 29
Office equipment and supplies, 98–105
    motion sensors and intercoms, 104
    run guards, 105
    sunscreens, 104, *104*
    telephone equipment and services, 102
    wall-mounted scheduler, 99–101
Older dogs, tips for handling, 129
On-leash, keeping dog, 32
Outdoor drains, preventing leaves or snow from, *133*, 135
Outdoor run
    dividers, 63–65
    entering, *134*
Out-of-towners, 170–71
Outside-run overhead fencing, 65–66
Overbooking, 122–23, 160
    avoiding, 122–23
Overhead fan, *61*
Owner
    brutality from, handling, 183

heeding information from, 178
    visitation rights during training, 38, 169

P

Paranoia, inducing in dog, 32
Parvo, dog with, 169
Payment, problem with collecting, 157–58
Perimeter fencing, 72–74
Playtoy, 30–31
Poisoning, first aid for, 191
Policies and practices, 121–44
    attitude, 142–44
    cleaning and disinfecting, 132–35
    client issues, 121–25
    dog issues, 125–27
    general business, 135–42
Porcupine quills, first aid for, 191
Praising your dog, 31–32, 39–40
Pregnant female, boarding a, 170
Privacy of clients, respecting, 124
Problems and solutions, 155–72
Puppy(ies)
    breeders' considerations, 24–32
    feeding, 24–25
    obedience class, 29
    praising, 31–32
    protection of, 32
    when to board, 126
"Puttering around" in the kennels, 126

R

Rabies, dog in quarantine period, 170
Rain, bringing dog in from run, 168
Rate, increasing your, 159
Receipts for payment, 118–19
Record keeping, 16, 40, 114, 145–54
    annual net gain/loss, 150
    basic bookkeeping, 146

charge accounts, 151–52
computerizing, 114
expense, 148–50
income, 146–48
of initial construction
costs, 16
of owner visits, 169
preferences, 150–51
seeking professional help,
153, 154
travel expenses, 153–54
utilities expenses, 153
Refrigeration, 60
Refusing to come inside, how
to handle dog, 168–69
Repairing or improving
kennels, 135
Reservations, 107–9
Roofing, 15, 58
of doghouse, 15
Run
avoiding catch on dog
collar, 111
construction of, 9–13
dividers, 63–64
fencing materials, 12
gates, 66
guards, 105
quantity of, 9–10
sample floor plan for, 51, 52
size of, 10, 46–47
surface, 10–12, 67–68
weather and, 51
Running fits, first aid for,
191

S

Sad dog, 194–95
Season, dogs in, 125–26, 167
Second line for phone, 103
Security, 8–9
basic boundaries, 8–9
countermeasures for
tunnelers, 9
considering when design-
ing the kennel, 50
exterior lighting, 60
equipment, 95
Separate meters, installing,
153
Shelving, 92
Shock, first aid for, 191

Sign, 76–77
Size of kennel, determining,
46–49
Skunks, first aid for, 191
Smokers, avoiding, 40, 136
Snacks, how to feed dog,
131–32
Special conditions or needs
by boarding dogs,
123
Sprains, first aid for, 191
Squeegees, 96, 97
Stool eating by dog, 166
Subletting, avoiding,
121–22
Sunscreens, 104, 104
Sympathy card, sending
out, 89, 127

T

Talking to dog, 135
Teasing of pet, avoiding, 32
Telephone equipment and
services, 102–5
answering machine or
service, 102–3
call-waiting, 103
cellular phone, 103
cordless phone, 102
second line, 103
Ten Commandments from
Canis software pro-
gram, 33
Thieves
being aware of, 162,
163–64
reaction to, 172
Ticks, first aid for, 192
Time inconvenience, due to
client, 160
Torsion, 128
Trainers, considerations for,
33–41
Training
contract, sample, 37
graduation from, 38–39
hints, 39–40
owner visitation rights
during, 38
record, sample, 36
skipping when ill, 171
yard, 34–35

Travel expenses, record
keeping of, 153–54
Trees, incorporating into
design, 53
Trough, outdoor clean-out,
69
Tying dog, 9, 32

U–V

Undercharging client, 159
Unknown dog, 177
Unruly dog, 167–68
Utilities expenses, record
keeping of, 153

Vacation time, 142
Vaccinations, recording,
112
Veterinarian
choosing a, 140
courses from a, 169
when to take boarder to,
126, 166, 170
who's paying, 164, 170
Videotaping dog's training,
41
Vomiting, first aid for, 192

W–Z

Wall-mounted scheduler,
99–101
Walls, 53–54
Waste disposal, 13, 68–72
Water for dog
checking, 130
placing in indoor run, 116
Water-related supplies, 91
Weather, considering
when designing the
kennel, 51
"What if" scenarios, 155–72
Whelping area, 20–21
Windbreak of doghouse
Windows, 54
Winter, special duties dur-
ing, 135
Wire mesh fencing, 73
Word of mouth about busi-
ness, 88
Worms, first aid for, 192

Zoning restrictions, 45–46